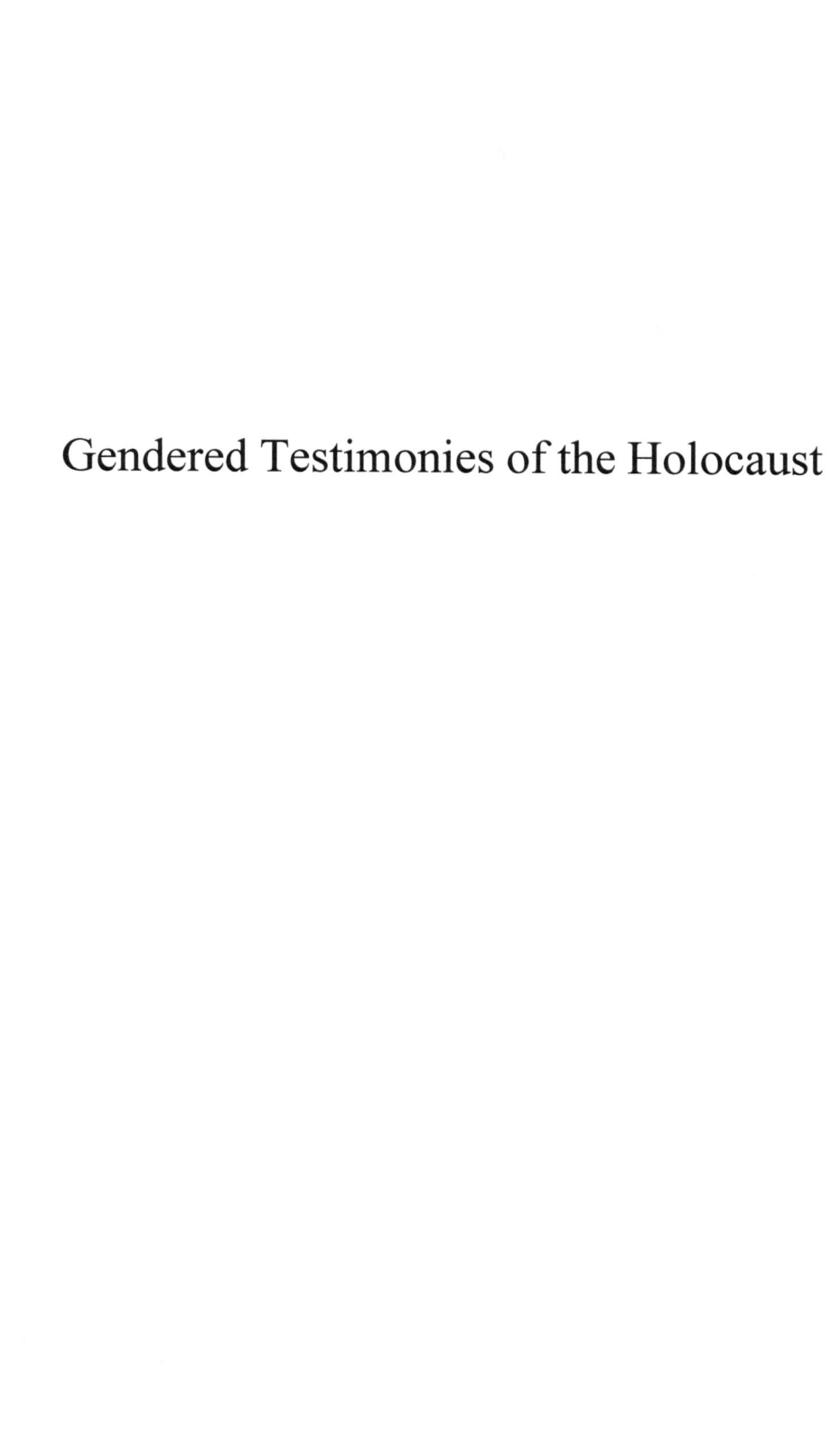

# Gendered Testimonies of the Holocaust

# Gendered Testimonies
# of the Holocaust

## *Writing Life*

### Petra M. Schweitzer

LEXINGTON BOOKS
Lanham • Boulder • New York • London

Published by Lexington Books
An imprint of The Rowman & Littlefield Publishing Group, Inc.
4501 Forbes Boulevard, Suite 200, Lanham, Maryland 20706
www.rowman.com

Unit A, Whitacre Mews, 26-34 Stannary Street, London SE11 4AB

British Library Cataloguing in Publication Information Available

**Library of Congress Cataloging-in-Publication Data**

Names: Schweitzer, Petra, author.
Title: Gendered testimonies of the Holocaust: writing life / Petra Schweitzer.
Description: Lanham ; Boulder : Lexington Books, 2015. | Includes bibliographical references and index.
Identifiers: LCCN 2015046065 (print)| LCCN 2015046588 (ebook)| ISBN 9780739190074 (cloth : alk. paper) | ISBN 9780739190081 (Electronic)
Subjects: LCSH: Holocaust, Jewish (1939-1945), in literature. | Holocaust, Jewish (1939-1945)--Personal narratives--History and criticism. | Jewish women in the Holocaust. | Holocaust survivors.
Classification: LCC PN56.H55 S30 2015 (print) | LCC PN56.H55 (ebook) | DDC 809/.93358405318--dc23 LC record available at http://lccn.loc.gov/2015046065

In Memory
of
Jacques Derrida and Emmanuel Levinas

# Contents

Permissions    ix

Acknowledgments    xi

Introduction    xiii

1  A Mother's Testimony as a Dwelling Place: *Dan Pagis*    1

2  Remembrance of the M/other/tongue: *Paul Celan*    21

3  The Maternal Function of Giving Testimony: *Charlotte Delbo*    49

4  Embodied Existence of Mothers: *Gisella Perl and Olga Lengyel*    69

Epilogue    85

Select Bibliography    89

Index    99

About the Author    103

# Permissions

# Acknowledgments

Writing this monograph was a deep and insightful experience. I remember the first moments of engaging with the testimonial works of Paul Celan, Charlotte Delbo, Olga Lengyel, Gisella Perl, and Dan Pagis. From the beginning of thinking, researching, planning, preparing, writing, and revising, I became absorbed in the scholarship of exceptional researchers, colleagues, institutions, friends, family members, and people with whom I talked about the texts, the authors, and the topic. I remember only too well my conversation with a student from Israel whom I met in the cafeteria of the Staatsbibliothek in Munich during my sabbatical in spring of 2014. In passing, we discussed Celan's visit to Israel and the student's experience of studying in Germany where members of his family had died in the death camps.

Rereading the works of Jacques Derrida and Emmanuel Levinas was a humbling experience, and the return to each line was stimulating for my work. While writing, I had always in mind that both philosophers were survivors of the Shoah. It was a privilege for me to meet R. Clifton Spargo's whose work on Levinas influenced my research and writing. His comments and editorial suggestions on several drafts before submitting the proposal taught me about writing, publication, and more about myself. I have deep admiration and gratitude to Robert E. Ehrenreich whose support went beyond any conventional sense of collegial involvement. His interest and involvement in projects regarding the remembrance of the Holocaust are legendary. His mentorship goes back to the time of my graduate studies at Emory, and his encouragement for this book kept me going.

I want to thank Steven Feldman from the Book Publication Office at the United States Holocaust Memorial Museum who reviewed the proposal I sent to my publisher. I am deeply grateful to Raina Kostova for listening to my ideas and her astute feedback during the entire process. She took the time to read my chapters and pointed to where some ideas were not clear enough. Dorota Glowacka gave of her passion and encouragement in support of this project. I thank my former advisor Cathy Caruth whose important work on literature and trauma I have long admired. I am thankful to Dalia Judovitz for her intellectual curiosity about my ideas and theoretical questions. My special thanks go to Deborah Lipstadt for her ongoing interest in my work. Judy Gerson listened to my developing thoughts when we met at the annual Conferences for Jewish

Studies. Leah Wolfson gave her support to the growing manuscript. I owe a great deal to Gina Daddario and Amy Sarch for their unfailing support during the writing process.

I thank the Jack, Joseph, and Morton Mandel Center for Advanced Holocaust Studies at the United States Holocaust Memorial Museum for supporting my research by making it possible for me to attend two Jack and Anita Hess Seminars for Faculty. It was a privilege for me to be part of the stimulating conversations with all members of the workshops. The resources at the museum have been indispensible to me.

I also would like to thank Shenandoah University for supporting my research.

My greatest debts are to Margit Meissner for sharing invaluable insights with my students at the museum and to the late Hugo Judovitz. Both are Holocaust survivors.

I am indebted to Adama Dieng for his dialogues and inspiration on genocide prevention.

Many thanks to my editor Regina Longo for her editorial support as well as the acquisitions editor Sarah Craig. I am particularly indebted to Robert Grogg for his assistance. I am grateful to the reviewers for their thoughtful and insightful comments that guided my revisions.

A number of friends encouraged, listened, commented, and urged me to persevere over the years. At the risk of leaving someone out, let me list them: Hamish Caldwell, Ann Grogg, Stefanie Harris, Mary and Warren Hofstra, Angela Hunter, Francisco Irianni, Beatrice Leis, Brian McGrath, James Mensch, Birgit and Detlef Nowak, Gabi Oberwinder, Stuart Romm, Peter Rosenbaum, Dale Aquino Sawaya and Richard Sawaya, Lissa Skitolsky, Brigitte and Richard Smith, Verena von Gagern-Steidle, Apostolos Vasilakis, and Barbara Weber. Friends in Munich and Paris, all artists, who individually felt close to the themes I was writing about, inspired me during a number of deep conversations: Fritz Hörauf, Tamara Ralis, Klaus Voswinckel (a writer and filmmaker who knew Paul Celan personally and wrote the first doctoral thesis about his complete works), and Jochen Winter.

I would like to thank my aunt Dorothea Fries, and my cousins Roland and Wolfhard Fries for their genuine interest in my manuscript. I am deeply grateful to my brother Bernd Schweitzer for supporting me in innumerable ways, particularly after my mother's death.

As always, my work stands upon the shoulders and is based upon encouragement and suggestions from colleagues, friends, and family. Any mistakes, however, are my responsibility.

# Introduction

The sense of survival as perhaps its own ethical code has long centered the study of Holocaust testimony, literature, and art. Terrence Des Pres's study *The Survivor: An Anatomy of Life in the Death Camps* (1976) provided the foundation for understanding survival as the most basic imperative of testimony emerging from the literature of the camps.[1] As scholars concentrated increasingly on the problem of representation in literary and artistic works about the Holocaust, they sometimes argued that the aesthetic dimension of representation competed with testimonial imperatives. Recently, critical insights developed through the field of gender studies have been incorporated into the conversation about Holocaust testimony and representation. Even as we have been encouraged to see gender itself as a construct, as a representation defined by social conventions, we have become fascinated by the influence of this construct on the act of representation in Holocaust testimony and art. The play of gender persists whether the testimonial texts in question specifically address women's memories and women's experiences, or whether they can come from male authors and speak from a position of masculinity unacknowledged by the authors, who necessarily put forth deeply gendered representations.

*Gendered Testimonies of the Holocaust: Writing Life* begins with the premise that writing proves virtually synonymous with survival, bearing the traces of life and of death carried within those who survived the atrocities of the Nazis. I revisit the poetry and prose of Paul Celan (1920–1970), Charlotte Delbo (1913–1985), Olga Lengyel (1908–2001), Gisella Perl (1907–1988) and Dan Pagis (1930–1986) with special attention paid to the differences between writing among men and women. In this respect, I dedicate myself to a reading of multiple acts of Holocaust art and testimony as sites for specifically gendered representations. And despite the perceptible differences in male versus female writing—differences whose measure I take throughout the book—I argue that *"an unconditional affirmation of life"* is evident equally among men and women in these testimonial writings.[2]

Early in my teaching career as assistant professor at Shenandoah University, I learned the benefits of living near Washington, D.C. Visiting the U.S. capital was not limited to discovering the District's attractions but also of taking my students to the living memorial of the Holocaust. The many educational field trips to the museum seem to impact me more than my students. Each time I see the narrative history of the systematic and radical anti-Semitic persecution of the Jewish people and non-Jewish groups, the feeling to inspire younger generations in the work of remembrance evokes a profound dedication toward the commemoration of the victims.

*Gendered Testimonies of the Holocaust:* W*riting Life* aims to offer another view of the literature of the Shoah. As David G. Roskies and Naomi Diamant have argued in *Holocaust Literature: A History and Guide,* the Jewish catastrophe has produced literature that "comprises all forms of writing, both documentary and discursive, and in any language, that have shaped the public memory of the Holocaust and been shaped by it."[3] In the years after the events of the Holocaust, survivors have written literary stories to keep the memory of the ones who vanished alive. In thinking about the structure of my monograph and the decision of choosing the literary works for my readings, three criteria guided my choice. First, I remembered specific episodes through which I was exposed to these works and how the stories and the language profoundly touched me. Second, I wanted to read works by survivor writers from diverse countries that were written in different languages. Third, I was interested in the topic of motherhood reflected in the works of male and female survivors.

It is universally acknowledged that reading unfolds as a personal experience. I remember my first reading, and how the literary expressions of these specific individual and collective stories drew me into the suffering of personal experiences and human enslavement with the sadistic abuse of the Nazi perpetrators aimed at mass annihilation. These stories are accounts of an intimate personal history of internal and external experiences calling upon readers to step inside the space of their constructed memory. In her book *The Era of the Witness,* Annette Wieviorka writes: "At times, testimony is transformed into literature. It is often supposed that history is better transmitted by works of nonfiction."[4] Within the context of the vast amount of Holocaust literature, I was drawn toward the testimonial works of Paul Celan, Charlotte Delbo, Olga Lengeyl, Dan Pagis, and Gisella Perl. Their literary expressions have been my guiding force to explore these testimonial works once more. To further emphasize my focus on these specific works, I would like to point out memorable moments that led me to unfold these literary voices that have shaped the public memory of the Holocaust. For example, when John Felstiner, a prominent scholar on the work of Paul Celan, gave a lecture at Emory University, I was absorbed in Celan's poems trying to understand his unreadable language. After a conversation with Felstiner, he gave me a signed copy of his book *Paul Celan: Poet, Survivor, Jew.*[5] I will never forget his telling me: "You should write on Celan," and each time I read one of Celan's poems I hear his voice in my ear. Cathy Caruth, my dissertation advisor at Emory University, taught Charlotte Delbo's literary testimony,

*Auschwitz and After*, in a graduate course on trauma. I was so taken by Delbo's individual and collective poetic narratives about women in the concentration camps that I wanted to carry on her testimony through my scholarly work. How can a poem of six lines testify about the deportation and communicate so much through literary language without given precise historical details I asked myself when reading Dan Pagis's poem "Written in Pencil in the Sealed Railway-Car" for the first time. Sidra Dekoven Ezrahi's articles in her book *Booking Passage: Exile and Homecoming in the Modern Jewish Imagination* became a valuable source for a study on modern Jewish writers, in particular Dan Pagis and Paul Celan, by examining the private and historical trauma through poetic imagination.[6] Years later, at the bookstore of the Holocaust Museum, I discovered the eyewitnesses accounts *Five Chimneys* by Olga Lengyel and *I Was a Doctor in Auschwitz* by Gisella Perl. I felt compelled to gain further insights into the memoirs of the two women's forced labor in Auschwitz while facing the inhuman orders given by Dr. Josef Mengele and the most notorious female SS guard Irma Grese. It was shattering to read these stories of violence to pregnant women, their newborn babies, and of a historical role that forced these two women to face the animalistic and ongoing evil actions of Dr. Mengele and Grese. My interest in women and the Holocaust was shaped by these two memoirs written shortly after the liberation of the camps. These stories allowed me to bridge the gap between history, artistic expression, and commemoration. Faced with the challenges to engage with the memorial story and realizing my intimate bond with each narrative, I was dumbfounded by the creative process involved in bringing these testimonial writings into the light of day but concluded that literary expressions ultimately represent an archetype of life after survival.

Writers write because they are inspired, they usually do not use any method, particularly not so, when under duress. The same applies to readers. They are drawn to the inspiration evoked by a text. Of all the possible texts a person could choose to read, something almost unknown draws the reader to a certain text. My assumption is that a resonance field magnetizes a reader to a text that stimulates in oneself an affinity to something one does not know, but feels drawn to read and, thereby, experience. The chosen text conjures and formulates something subliminal that the reader possibly carries within himself, via the collective unconscious, in which everyone takes part to various degrees. What is lying dormant in the reader becomes conscious through following the imagery contained in the words of the poet or writer. Why we are attracted to certain texts and not others remains as much a mystery, as does the secret of inspiration causing a literary work to be born. In reading, each poetic testimony appeared transparent echoing the inner life of each individual survivor-writer, and with it reflecting the dimension of the historical time. It seems that the survivor writers had the capacity to come to a level that might have been a surprise even for them. To experience the profound message of each writer, one has to have a different openness to approach the truthfulness in these pieces of artistic works. Therefore, it was not my intention to chronologically present the corpus of their testimonies, but to dive into the unknown history experienced during and after the Shoah. In reading each work, I pondered over the question: How was it possible for these survivors to write about human destruction, if death is such an intimate part of the survivors' survival? It is a well-known fact that they have taken upon themselves the responsibility for the dead to tell what they cannot testify anymore. Yet, how was it possible for the men and women to constitute such works in the midst of surviving the genocide? What turns writing into a vital memory the moment a reader starts reading? Time and again the writers envision and produce their writings as nothing less than acts of survival.

This is not to be taken for granted in Holocaust testimony. Many scholars—perhaps most noteworthy among them Lawrence Langer—have long argued an opposite position, emphasizing that Holocaust testimony speaks from a position so alien to ordinary life as to negate rather than affirm the usual features of existence.[7] In conversation with the diverse ways in which "survival" has been construed in the field of Holocaust studies, I began *Gendered Testimonies of the Holocaust* from Jacques Derrida's conception of survival as the unconditional affirmation of life. In an interview given to *Le Monde* shortly before his death, Derrida admitted that he never learned to live, if only because this would have required that he learn to die. To take mortality into account is for Derrida to experience life as survival. At last facing his mortality, Derrida asserts in his last interview: "[Survival] constitutes the very structure of what we call existence." In Derrida's view, "a complication of the life-death opposition proceeds in me from an unconditional affirmation of life. Survival, this is life after life, life more than life, the most intense life possible." I chart Derrida's concept of survival as an opposition between life and death as proceeding from the oddly paired connotations of "an unconditional affirmation of life" and "living the most intense life possible."[8] Finding a double meaning in survival, Derrida emphasizes Walter Benjamin's distinction between *überleben* (which is to live after death, as a book can survive the death of its author or a child endure the death of parents), and *fortleben* (which is to continue to live)—and the play between those two emphases in survival is something I explore throughout the book.[9]

Though he died of a terminal disease, Derrida encountered his mortality under natural conditions. This is in sharp contrast to the lived reality of mortality in the camps, specifically, the daily methodical violence meted out by the Nazis against the Jewish people. Victims of the Holocaust were forced to apprehend their mortality under the most inhuman conditions. The Nazi attempt to annihilate European Jewry meant that the perpetrators, through their systemically dehumanizing tyranny, prevented victims from having an identity or from retaining basic human values in the face of anonymous death. For those victims who somehow survived the Nazi terror, life emerged again only through the encounter with death. As Jean François Lyotard says, "The word 'survivor' implies that a being who is dead or should have died is still living."[10] According to Lyotard, the survivor must always be either a witness or a victim. This notion helps provide a bridge from Derrida's conception of survival and my exploration of survival in testimonies that emerge from the context of the camps.

Another way in which I construct the theoretical bridge between literary testimonies of Celan, Delbo, Lengyel, Pagis, and Perl emerging from the Holocaust and Derrida's conceptual framework for survival is by invoking Derrida's personal history, specifically, his childhood experience of Jewishness as survival. Born an Algerian Jew, Derrida was a subject of, and shaped by, Vichy's *Statut des juifs* of 1940 and suffered the persecution of the Jewish people, in particular the anti-Jewish violence enacted in Algeria. He was subjected to the loss of his French citizenship and expulsion from school.[11] Derrida himself acknowledges the extent to which the memory of exclusion is intimately related to his work as he theorizes the "trace" even by writing against the effacement of traces: "I would not need to write otherwise; my writing is not in the first place a philosophical writing or that of an artist, even if, in certain cases, it might look like that or take over from these other kinds of writing."[12] It was his deepest conviction that his first desire was not to produce a philosophical work or a work of art, but rather to preserve memory. Fundamentally, then, Derrida construes the relation between *life* and *survival* as the act of writing, and conceives all language as an act of memory.

In a similar way, the works of these survivors arise creatively from a vigorous spark, the desire to preserve memory. Testimony for each of these writers is a form of relation to oneself but also to others. It situates each survivor's anguish in writing as a need to write so as to affirm life. Writing as such always bears witness to the life of the one who should be dead by now and thus to the miracle of having survived. My claim, elaborated over the course of *Gendered Testimonies of the Holocaust*, is that the act of writing testimony manifests itself as the most intensive form of life possible. Encountering the relation between *life* and *survival,* I suggest that writing symbolizes the act of giving birth. The figure of birth-giving can be seen in relation to the Nazis' policy with respect to an explicit philosophical problem: namely, the objectification of subjects into numbers and the inhuman experiments on human beings. Writing as the symbolized act of giving birth is thus reconstructing the subjects' identity. In the face of having been labeled as inferior nonexistent humans, and therefore the metaphorical birth in relation to creating a memorial life for the dead is embodied in each testimonial account. In so doing, the new identity of the subject takes place from a point outside the autonomous

subject, that is, the subject does not turn its reflection on the self but on the other. As a result, writing itself is twofold: 1) in its recuperative function, writing reestablishes the survivor writers identity and 2) this new identity emerges as an essential constituent of the subject's subjectivity linked to the responsibility of "the Other." Following an inner call and to take responsibility testifying for the ones who are dead, the self-breaks with the Descartes's cogito: "I think therefore I am."[13] This conditioned identity of the survivors provides the possibility of an ethical relationship with another.

The intrinsic care for the other has been described in the philosophical writings of Emmanuel Levinas. Based on his concept of subjectivity in which the subject is responsible for the other makes an ethical relationship possible. Identity is by definition always formed in relation to another, as the survivor speaks from an individual experience inextricably linked with others. Writing affirms the most intensive life by inscribing the inextricable relation between the self and the other as part of writing's act of survival. If writing symbolizes the act of giving birth, then, writing itself takes on the metaphorical role of motherhood, that is, the survivor as the one who writes, re-creates a new subject identity that is also embedded within the act of giving life to another.

The monograph bearing most directly on my own work is Dorota Glowacka's *Disappearing Traces: Holocaust Testimonials, Ethics, and Aesthetics.*[14] Her profound work foregrounds the role of language in mediating trauma and the sometimes contrary imperatives of the aesthetic versus the ethical orientation in the work of arts. Glowacka's theoretical insights and readings emerge out of Levinas's concept of subjectivity in which the ethical subject is positioned. In coining the term "subjectivity as the structure of witnessing," Glowacka examines literary testimonies to explore the different modes of representation that produce new idioms such as "memory phrase" or "memory event" stressing the relation between the ethical and the aesthetic phrase.[15] Although her compelling work underlies my readings, my thesis takes a different kind of approach. It is through the act of writing itself that survivor-writers first reconstruct their identity. It emerges as the most intensive life, and through the affirmation of life makes the ethical relationship toward the other possible. My own work is continuous with the rigorously interdisciplinary work of recent scholars such as Michael Rothberg, Robert Eaglestone, Brett Ashley Kaplan, and Henry Pickford.[16] And yet no study of Holocaust literature, art, and philosophy has yet to formulate the thesis on which my book concentrates, specifically, that writing within the context of the Holocaust—broadly interpreted to include all modes of artistic expression—constitutes itself as an act of survival with its own peculiar ethical qualities.

More specifically, my exploration of writing's affirmation of life and assertion of identity focuses on the gendered dimension of expression and language. As I consider the gendered dimension of testimony to explore the difference in writing by male and female survivors, I ask, what kind of writing defines each female and male writer? And how do the specifics of male versus female writing factor into or force me to alter my basic premise that writing is generated, even in the context of the Holocaust, as the unconditional affirmation of life?

*Gendered Testimonies of the Holocaust* does not engage in the binary structure of gender and the hierarchically constructed roles in terms of privileging the male over the female. The criteria that guided my discussion on *Gendered Testimonies* emerge out of Levinas's concept of maternity. What is the relationship between self and the other in relation to his notion of maternity? At the very heart of this elaboration on motherhood lies not the physical relationship between mother and child but the ethical relation to the other. What is the relationship between self and the other in relation to Levinas's notion of maternity? In her article: "From Eros to Maternity: Love, Death and 'the Feminine' in the Philosophy of Emmanuel Levinas,"[17] Claire Katz investigates in the theme of death and knowledge in the Western tradition in reference to Levinas's ethical thought on subjectivity. She examines the philosopher's concept in relation to his critics arguing that the philosopher characterizes in *Otherwise and Being* "the feminine" as maternity.[18] The cornerstone of his idea "demonstrates a shift from the priority of death to the priority of life, where life is linked to responsibility for the other."[19] At stake is the death of the other and the responsibility for the other which at the same time inverts the masculine to the feminine. Undermining the implicit masculine tenor within the tradition, she underscores the notion that the general view of death, life, and philosophy has not succeeded in becoming any closer to another person. She goes on to explain: "Human subjectivity has been defined in terms of freedom, independence, and knowledge."[20] Exploring the works of Plato, Socrates, and Heidegger, Katz discusses how Levinas's ethics confronts the Western tradition philosophical quest for death and knowledge by replacing the concern for one's own death with the concern for the other's death. Katz also notes how Levinas's understanding of subjectivity is transformed from one who is free to the one who is obligated, and therefore is always already intersubjective, and always already ethically accountable.[21] What Levinas means by this is the inextricable and asymmetrical relationship between the ethical subject and the other.

By focusing on the significance of Levinas's concept of maternity, Katz points out that the metaphor not only derived from the relationship between mother and child. Referring to his essay "No Identity," Katz describes the philosopher's reading of the biblical term (*rakhamin*) goes back to the word for uterus (*rekem*): "*Rakhamim* is the relation of the uterus to the *other*, whose gestation takes place within it."[22] Katz goes on to explain that Levinas's focus on the womb means maternity "as it applies to women—gestation and birth the image is nonetheless instructive." [23] If maternity positions the self in relation to the other into a feminine bodily existence, then, the questions can be raised: How are gender differences reflected within the testimonial writing? What interests me in Levinas's metaphorical thinking, as elaborated in Katz's article, is the fact that men and women can equally become a maternal body carrying the other. Thus, *Gendered Testimonies of the Holocaust: Writing Life* depends upon the survivor-writers' new life and the embodiment of the others' life with the textual space of each works. In bringing together Derrida's concept of "an unconditional affirmation of life" Levinas's idea on maternity where life is linked to responsibility for the other, I focus on the embedding images of motherhood in the ethical relation between survivor-writers and the other.

In this book's four chapters, the works of the male and female survivor-writers create a textual space that metaphorically carries the other in the maternal body into life. As discussed earlier, Levinas's notion of maternity views the subject, masculine and feminine, equally within the maternal body. Since maternity employed as metaphor exceeds the biological aspects of maternity, I explore the images of motherhood in relation to the affirmation of life beyond death.

As I argue throughout the book, the most profound—and painful— experiences are transformed into words. As the study further explores the difference between male and female writing in the context of the Holocaust, it asks how the poetic dimension of language bears on life and also bears up life in the face of death. And much as the insights into identity developed through pioneering works in Gender Studies advance our understanding of Holocaust testimony, my lifelong work in Holocaust Studies and my new perspective on Holocaust testimony and language open an avenue for thinking about how and to what extent the "affirmation of life" underlies all of our gendered constructs of identity.

The theoretical framework of the book is informed by such thinkers as Jacques Derrida, Emmanuel Levinas, and Jean-François Lyotard.[24] By engaging these foundational philosophical texts, I explore the core relation between survival and writing through the lens of literary works. I focus on the issue of language not only as a vehicle for transmitting traumatic memory but also as a medium through which writing manifests itself as a living commitment to reconstruct one's life. In other words, I explore the issue of survival and affirmation of life as an utterance in relation to the other. Memory, as a dynamic between *inside* and *outside*, is marked within each of these individual poetic writings.[25] As I address the ways in which Delbo, Lengyel, and Perl describe a state of powerlessness dependent on specific abuses of the female body within the context of the camps, I draw attention to the female body as the site and vehicle of women's experiences. In feminine writing, the allegorized figure of the female body embodies both life and death. These writers construct the

women's body primarily as a source of life, invoking the r
as that which carries a new life, and thereafter by an a(
renaming the woman's body as a discursive tool that pres..
of all the dead women. By contrast, in the male writing of Ce1a.
Pagis, I focus on the tendency of these testimonies to interrogate the
structures of "patriarchal" hierarchy and domination experienced as the
daily tyranny of life in the camps. As Celan and Pagis deploy the trope of
motherhood as the very sign of creation, they embed the maternal presence within the poetic voice. "Gender is thus somewhat arbitrary in all
languages," as Barbara Johnson reminds us, "but that arbitrariness may
nevertheless have an unconsciously internalized referential effect."[26] So
in Celan's "Sprich auch Du," *die Muttersprache* (the mother tongue)
proves fundamental to the creative possibility of poetic voice; and in
Pagis's poetry as a female voice, such as that allegorized as Eve in "Written in Pencil in the Sealed Railway-Car," is that which can appeal to the
world outside the railcar. Thus, in female as well as male writing, the
figure of the mother's voice describes the poetic voice as that which elucidates the will to love or the affirmation of life.

In the concentration camps, the daily life of victims unfolded as a
daily struggle between life and death. Deprived of a world *outside,* life
was at stake every moment. Dori Laub, a child survivor of the Holocaust,
describes the space of dehumanization as a world *inside:* "There was no
longer another to which one could say "Thou" in the hope of being
heard, of being recognized as a subject, of being answered."[27] No appeal
to the Other was possible, he tells us. The unimaginable horrors of methodical yet arbitrary torture and killing defined the lives of those who
survived these terrors. For survivors, the sufferings internalized during
those years becomes the motivation to address a world *outside,* testifying
to what happened when no one could hear their cries. There are no resources left to them, other than their own internal experiences from a
world *inside.* This is a fundamental part of survival, and *Gendered Testimonies of the Holocaust* explores such issues as inscribed within each testimony, considering the intersection of trauma, testimony, and language in
the lived reality and affirmed life of the survivor.

Much of the critical literature on the modern subject bears witness to a
thinking self that represents itself cognitively, framing its existence for a
world outside. Perhaps the strongest critique of that model comes from
Emmanuel Levinas, who provides a new framework for understanding
the survivor's necessity to construct a new self. In *Totality and Infinity,*
Levinas posits the self's unique responsibility for the other person, who
emerges from a sentient existence as a separate, independent self "who
stands outside of the social and historical order." The sense of urgency in
the self to testify—and to testify in writing about what they survived in
the Nazi camps—attests to this truth of the ethical relation as described
by Levinas. Though Levinas himself is often skeptical of writing and

epresentation, I pursue the underlying meaning of survival as affirmation in the context of those who are "writing life." In my take on Levinas, then, an affirmation of life is implicit in the separate, independent self, and it becomes apparent only via the unique responsibility for the Other that arises from the act of giving testimony.

In my formulation, life determines itself as affirmation of life by giving testimony. As indicated, this premise of my book is derived in part from Derrida's conceptualization of survival as "the unconditional affirmation of life."

But I am taking up that claim in a context that threatens to undo it at every turn. How do we understand the notions of "the unconditional affirmation of life" and of living "the most intensive life possible" when applying such propositions to those who survived the most inhuman of conditions, conditions created by their Nazi persecutors? How do these survivors affirm life after surviving the attempt at the systemic negation of their lives as valuable or meaningful?

Derrida takes up the theme of affirmation in his essay "Ulysses Gramophone."[28] There he explores the connotation of the doubled "yes" arising from Ulysses's "yes, yes." The first "yes" happens in the moment of picking up the phone, as one affirms that, yes, I can hear the other before actually speaking. The second "yes" affirms the other to myself, in the moment of acknowledging that my response is about to come. In applying this paradigm to writing as the "unconditional affirmation of life," I perceive a "yes" not only in the affirmation of the other to myself but also in the responsibility I take for the other, as exemplified in the writing of an event that has already happened. On my reading, Derrida's affirmation resonates with and extends Levinas's notion of the true vocation of ethical subject as for-the-other.

All of this is argued against the background of those nagging questions—so fundamental to the field of Holocaust Studies—about the impossibility of representing the event. Famously, Jean-François Lyotard frames the problem as follows: "The unstable state and instant of language wherein something which must be put into phrases cannot yet be," and so "one *must* inscribe in words and images."[29] In confronting impossibility, Lyotard insists that one cannot escape the necessity of representation, a representation that shatters all representations. Such a formulation brings us to the threshold of traumatic experience.

Trauma underlies or frames all these narratives. As someone who trained with Cathy Caruth at Emory, I am indebted to her influence in the field of trauma studies, most notably in her books *Unclaimed Experience, Literature in the Ashes of History* and the edited version of *Trauma: Exploration in Memory.*[30] My present understanding of testimony as survival viewed with other models of trauma as the locus for understanding testimony, witness, and memory put forward by Herman Langbein, in *People in Auschwitz*; by Ann Kaplan, in *Trauma Culture: The Politics of Terror and Loss in Media and Literature* and Michael S. Roth's *Memory, Trauma and History: Essays on Living with the Past;* by Agi Rubin and Henry Greenspan, in *Reflections: Auschwitz, Memory, and a Life Recreated* and finally by Simone Gigliotti, in *The Train Journey: Transit, Captivity, and Witnessing the Holocaust* have influenced my research.[31] My book's overarching premise—that writing as survival is ineradicably an affirmation of life—involves an interpretive take on a long tradition of studies on testimony and language in the context of the Holocaust, beginning perhaps most fundamentally with Shoshana Felman's and Dori Laub's *Testimony: Crises of Witnessing in Literature, Psychoanalysis, and History.*[32]

In the formation of phrases, each writer or poet studied here also points to the fragmentation of representation. Nevertheless, each bears witness to survival itself, to the effort to put words and images into phrases. In choosing primarily literary testimonies—by Paul Celan, Dan Pagis, Charlotte Delbo, Olga Lengyel, and Gisella Perl—I concentrate on poetic works in which the writers identify themselves as Holocaust survivors and also as Jewish or as a member of the French resistance such as Charlotte Delbo. Each individual text also marks a fundamental scar in reference to individual or collective suffering. As I examine each of these literary works in terms of its figurative language rooted in the relation between absence and presence, I am focusing on the very capacity of language as testimony to articulate that which memory cannot readily enact. The complicated relation to memory gives great importance to figurative language in my study, and justifies the special attention paid to poetry here. In different ways, I argue, the figures that are central to each writer serve to communicate the challenge of remembering and transmitting the history of the Holocaust. In what ways, I ask of each poet, can we hear the voice of the survivor in the here and now? How does literary language bring us into the now, and into a face-to-face encounter with the unspeakable crime of mass death? Ultimately, how do these writers reflect on their experience of survival through an act of writing that—as survival—becomes a microcosm of the Holocaust itself?

Among the different texts, there is an interesting similarity in relation to questions of gender. I draw further parallels between Celan and Pagis as men who suffered the Nazi forced labor camps and Delbo and Lengyel as women who survived Auschwitz. My inquiry into their literary testimonies is motivated by the difference in writing. What are the patterns of writing that speak to a deeper recurring phenomenon in gender constitution? Was it the historical influence that inspired Celan and Pagis to write poetry? What causes these female survivors to write narrative prose and the male survivor to write poetry?

Sara R. Horowitz's book *Voicing the Void: Muteness in Holocaust Fiction* presents important research addressing the ways in which memory has been conveyed through literature and visual text.[33] Her focus on the theme of muteness as an indispensible part of language after the Shoah has been an insightful resource for this book.[34]

Over the last fifteen years, the field of Holocaust Studies has become truly interdisciplinary. My own work in the field has been informed by and in dialogue with a great many excellent recent studies on literature, art, ethics, and testimony. *Gendered Testimonies* charts new territory in each of these areas. From my perspective, the wave of interest in the philosophy of Emmanuel Levinas and Jacques Derrida, and the relevance of these thinkers to the study of the Holocaust, has especially energized the field in recent years.

Perhaps closest to my own interests, however, are the works by R. Clifton Spargo, *Vigilant Memory: Emmanuel Levinas, the Holocaust, and the Unjust Death* and the edited collection with Robert M. Ehrenreich *After Representation? The Holocaust, Literature and Culture* which ask us to consider how ontology or our language for ethics and shifting cultural context for representation might be altered after the Holocaust.[35] Since my study examines the testimonies from the perspective of gender, identity, and hierarchical male authorship, Sarah R. Horowitz's *Voicing the Void: Muteness and Memory in Holocaust Fiction*, Myrna Goldenberg and Amy Shapiro's edited collection *Different Horrors, Same Hell*,[36] or Susan Garner generated in the context of feminist reflections indispensable theories.[37] While Horowitz claims the differentiation of experience of male and female victims, Goldenberg's individual work focus on Jewish women and the different kind of humiliation, her collection with Amy Shapiro pays special attention to the different kind of humiliations in the camps. For example, Susan Garner's contributions to feminist theory and gender analysis discuss the oppressive gender roles in real life and literature. Theories of gender in the field of the Holocaust reflect not only different ideas in the social construction before, during, and after the Holocaust but also focus on the male oriented authorship.

In the first chapter, "A Mother's Testimony as a Dwelling Place," I examine the work of the Hebrew poet Dan Pagis (writing in Hebrew), in particular his poem "Written in Pencil in the Sealed Railway-Car" from his book *Points of Departure*.[38] Pagis explores the tenuous space of the railcar, a location in which personal and communal narratives intersect. What differentiates the poetic narrative from other literary testimonies is Pagis's rhetorical procedure evading any reference of experience. For this chapter, I will be drawing on Sidra DeKoven Ezrahi's book *Booking Passage: Exile and Homecoming in the Jewish Modern Imagination*.[39] The theoretical framework of this chapter returns to Derrida's concept of survival. For Pagis, a Romanian Jewish child survivor, the railcar contains the entirety of Jewish history—past, present, and future. His poetic narrative alludes to the first murderer in the history of humankind but exacerbates the biblical reference. Eve, who is trapped with her son Abel inside the railcar leaves a message behind addressing a universal "you" to tell something to her first-born son Cain absent in the sealed railcar. In this strain, I will engage with Derrida's notion of the trace as a form of pre-serving memory. Eve is a figure of all life (Genesis 3:20) who takes on the responsibility of telling her story to another unknown person. In inscrib-ing a message on the wall, Eve enables a transition from the "inside" of the cattle car to another (a possible reader) "outside" after death. The very condition of Eve's writing as a victim elicits Derrida's concept of survival in which life and death are inscribed in writing. Pagis's poetic narrative, I claim, bears witness to a life of all victims beyond their death. What is revealed through the poem is the possibility of a future reader. Reading the poem has an inherently ethical dimension because the reader cannot escape her/his presence "inside" the cattle car. The true power of the poem is due to the fact that the experience of reading is a vehicle that insists upon the affirmation of life past and present, and a future to come.

In the second chapter, "Remembrance of the M/other/tongue," I exam-ine Paul Celan's poem "Sprich auch Du" (Speak you too), I focus on Paul Celan's paradoxical relationship with German as his mother tongue and his lifelong struggle to write poetry again in the language of the murder-ers as reflected in particular passages of his 1958 Bremen Speech.[40] In drawing attention to the procedures of making aesthetic choices in the aftermath of the Shoah, I read the poem "Sprich auch Du," as an arche-type for writing a testimonial *poetics of survival*. In light of the poet's struggle with German *after* the Shoah, I read the apostrophic "Du," as the figure of the maternal voice. "Sprich auch Du," was published in a collec-tion of poems called *Von Schwelle zu Schwelle* (*From Threshold to Threshold*) in 1955, the second volume of Celan's early poetry after the Holocaust.[41] To what extent can the poem be read as an allegory of Celan's poetologi-cal reflection about his life in creating a poetics of survival?

In continuing the German language for purposes of remembrance, one could say, it is the female aspect of the poet's Jewishness that unfolds within the German. I explore the term of "artless art" as expressed in Celan's Meridian speech. The notion of "artless art" evoked by the most prominent Jewish German-speaking poet points to an ethical imperative in which the artist writes his poem embedded within the history of the Shoah. Celan's two important claims foreground his new poetic form that coincides with Derrida's concept of survival. Having survived the labor camps and the death of his parents in Romania during the war, Celan admits his uneasiness with the German language, yet emphasizes the necessity to continue writing as a poet: "Nothing in the world can make a poet stop writing poetry, even if he is Jewish and the language of his poems is German."[42] Almost twenty-four years after the fall of Nazi Ger-many, Celan makes a significant statement: "La poesie ne s'impose plus, elle s'expose." In an exemplary way, he articulates the shift in writing poetry. The emergence of a new concept, that is, the "poetry of exposi-tion," breaks with the previous literary accounts of the German traditions. Therefore, the poem must be examined through Celan's theoretical framework. For Celan, speech consists of an orality that can be present in the written word as well as in the spoken. And this orality, in fact, has better possibilities in writing than without writing. Hence, the poet responds to his own call in an artfully crafted poetic language committed to writing life. In its orality, such a language cannot violate but speaks of violation. In continuing to use the German language for purposes of remembrance, one could say, it is the female aspect of the poet's Jewishness that unfolds within the German. In writing, Celan provides a vibrant remembrance of the Shoah for preserving the life of his mother and millions of anonymous victims.

In the third chapter, "The Maternal Function of Giving Testimony," I explore the phenomenon of "prosthetic" language. In so doing, I investigate Charlotte Delbo's trilogy *Aucun de nous ne reviendra* (1970), in particular a story titled: "La jambe d'Alice" ("Alice's Leg").[43] Delbo, a non-Jewish survivor of the concentration camp and member of the French Resistance, constructs a story in which a wooden leg of a dead inmate becomes the center of attention. Alice, a prisoner of the death camps, died a long and lonely death in front of other female prisoners. Seeing a wooden leg in front of Block 25, Alice's friends are shocked but repeatedly return to the leg that seems to be alive. Drawing on Derrida's articulation of survival as "the unconditional affirmation of life," and Levinas's ethical subject, I demonstrate how Delbo's figurative imposition creates a living memory through a wooden leg. I argue that Alice's leg as a literary figure substitutes for the absence of the dead Alice's leg as a trace to remember the inhuman death of Alice. Drawing on Derrida's articulation of memory within language, I will discuss how Delbos's inanimate object becomes alive by remembering Alice and her inmate friends.

The last chapter, "Embodied Existence of Mothers," begins by discussing the memoirs of two Jewish survivors of the concentration camps, examining Gisella Perl's *I was a Doctor in Auschwitz* (1948), and Olga Lengyel, *Five Chimneys* (1947).[44] Both women narrate the violence of Nazi perpetrators and their destructive medical methods against (Jewish) women. Forced to assist the evil SS physician Josef Mengele, the two women describe his obsession to destroy the human body especially those of (Jewish) women, their unborn or newly born children, and the sadistic medical experiments, sterilization experiments in particular.

In feminist theories, the body has long been a disputed site in questions of gender. Fundamental questions such as "What is gender?" continue to evoke alternative discourse. I suggest that the essential question of "What is gender?" must be rethought in relation to the Nazis' systematic apparatus of destruction and annihilation as it operated on female bodies. What was it like to be a female (Jewish) prisoner in the concentration camp? It is within this framework that I will explore the relation between the dismemberment of the female body and the embodied nature of pain. How do we understand these testimonies in relation to the female body? What distinguishes the relationship between the physicians as victims themselves and the other women? In addition, I argue that the two memoirs construct what I call "the ethical body" through Perl's and Lengyel's responses to the meaningless suffering of the "other" (to use Levinas's term).

## NOTES

1. Terrence Des Pres, *The Survivor: An Anatomy of Life in the Death Camps* (New York: Oxford University Press, 1976).
2. Jacques Derrida, *Learning to Live Finally: The Last Interview*, trans. Pascale-Anne Brault and Michael Naas, introd. Jean Birnbaum, (New York: Melville House Publishing, 2007), 50. Originally published in French as *Apprendre à vivre enfin: Entretien avec Jean Birnbaum* (Paris: Éditions Galilée, 2005). The interview also appeared in *Le Monde*, August 19, 2004. See also Jacques Derrida, "Living On: Border Lines," in *Deconstruction and Criticism*, ed. Harold Bloom et al. (New York: Continuum, 1979), 62–142; Judith Butler "On Never Having Learned How to Live," *Differences* 16, no. 2 (2005): 27–34; Eduardo Cadava, "Remembering Jacques Derrida: Derrida's Futures," *Grey Room* 20 (Summer 2005): 74–79.
3. David G. Roskies and Naomi Diamant *Holocaust Literature. A History and Guide* (Waltham, MA: Brandeis University Press, 2012), 2.
4. Annette Wieviorka, *The Era of the Witness* (Ithaca and London: Cornell University Press, 2006), 22.
5. John Felstiner, *Paul Celan: Poet, Survivor, Jew* (New Haven and London: Yale University Press, 1995).
6. Sidra DeKoven Ezrahi, *Booking Passage: Exile and Homecoming in the Modern Jewish Imagination* (Berkeley and Los Angeles. University of California Press, 2000).
7. Lawrence Langer, *Holocaust Testimonies* (New Haven: Yale University, 1991).
8. Jacques Derrida, *Learning to Live Finally: The Last Interview*, 51.
9. Walter Benjamin, *Gesammelte Schriften* (Frankfurt: Suhrkamp, 1972–1989), 4: 10. See also Samuel Weber, *Benjamin's –abilities* (Cambridge, MA: Harvard University Press, 2008), 66–68, 79–94.
10. Jean-François Lyotard, "The Survivor," in *Towards the Postmodern*, ed. Robert Harvey and Mark S. Roberts (New York: Humanities Press, 1998). Originally published in French as *La Condition postmoderne: Rapport sur le savoir* (Paris: Les Editions de Minuit. 1979).
11. Jacques Derrida, *Jacques Derrida*, trans. Geoffrey Bennington (Chicago: University of Chicago Press, 1993). Originally published as *Circonfession* (Paris: Seuil, 1991).
12. Jacques Derrida, Points . . . *Interviews, 1974–1993*, ed. Elisabeth Weber, trans. Peggy Kamuf and others (Stanford: Stanford University Press: 1995), 143.
13. René Descartes, *Discourse on Method and the Meditations*, trans. F. E. Sutcliffe (Harmondsworth, UK: Penguin, 1979).
14. Dorota Glowacka, *Disappearing Traces: Holocaust Testimonials, Ethics, and Aesthetics* (Seattle and London: University of Washington Press, 2012).
15. Ibid., 14.
16. See Michael Rothberg, *Multidirectional Memory: Remembering the Holocaust in the Age of Decolonization* (Stanford: Stanford University Press, 2009); Robert Eaglestone, *The Holocaust and the Postmodern* (Oxford: Oxford University Press, 2004); and Brett Ashley Kaplan, *Unwanted Beauty: Aesthetic Pleasure in Holocaust Representation* (Chicago: University of Illinois Press, 2007). Theories of aesthetics that perceive affinity in the poetics of writing and the visual arts have been debated and argued by Shelley Hornstein et al., ed., *Impossible Images: Contemporary Art After the Holocaust* (New York: New

York University Press, 2003); Stephen Feinstein, *Absence/Presence: Critical Essays on the Artistic Memory of the Holocaust* (Syracuse: Syracuse University Press, 2005); Melissa Raphael, *Judaism and the Visual: a Post-Holocaust Theology of Jewish Art* (London and New York: Continuum International Publishing Group, 2009); and Nicholas Chare, *Auschwitz and Afterimages: Abjection, Witnessing and Representation* (London: I. B. Tauris Press, 2011).

17. Claire Katz, "From Eros to Maternity: Love, Death and 'the Feminine' in the Philosophy of Emmanuel Levinas," in *Women and Gender in Jewish Philosophy*, ed. Hava Tirosh-Samuelson. Jewish Literature and Culture (Bloomington: Indiana University Press, 2004), 153–75.

18. Ibid., 155. Katz points out that Levinas characterizes "the feminine," as eros in *Time and The Other*, as dwelling in *Totality and Infinity*, and finally in *Otherwise than Being: or Beyond Essence* as maternity.

19. Ibid., 156.

20. Ibid., 153.

21. Ibid., 154.

22. Ibid., 163–64.

23. Ibid., 164. Katz explains that Levinas's own reference to Isaiah indicates that he draws the image of maternity from the Hebrew Bible. Throughout Isaiah, the narrator refers to the image of the womb, and the experience of birth the most intimate bond between mother and child.

24. Jacques Derrida, *Learning to Live Finally: The Last Interview; Monolingualism of the Other, or, The Prosthesis of Origin*, trans. Patrick Mensah (Stanford: Stanford University Press, 1998); *Sovereignties in Question*, ed. Thomas Dutoit and Outi Pasanen (New York: Fordham University Press, 2005); Emmanuel Levinas, *Totality and Infinity: An Essay on Exteriority*, trans. Alphonso Lingis (Pittsburgh: Duquesne University Press, 1998); *Otherwise than Being, or Beyond Essence*, trans. Alphonso Lingis (Pittsburgh: Duquesne University Press, 1998); "Useless Suffering," in *Entre Nous: Thinking-of-the-Other* (New York: Columbia University Press, 1998); *Is it righteous to be? Interviews with Emmanuel Levinas*, ed. Jill Robbins (Stanford: Stanford University Press, 2002); Jean-François Lyotard, *The Differend: Phrases in Dispute*, trans. Georges Van Den Abbeele (Minneapolis: University of Minnesota Press, 1988; *Heidegger and "the Jews,"* trans. Andreas Michel and Mark S. Roberts (Minneapolis: University of Minnesota Press, 1990).

25. The topic of the *inside* and *outside* is a repeated theme in Holocaust Literature.

26. Ibid., 23.

27. Dori Laub, "An Event Without a Witness: Truth, Testimony and Survival," in *Testimony: Crisis of Witnessing in Literature, Psychoanalysis, and History*, ed. Shoshana Felman and Dori Laub, (New York and London: Routledge, 1992), 82.

28. Jacques Derrida, "Ulysses Gramophone: Hear Say Yes in Joyce," trans. François Raffoul, ed. Derek Attridge, in *Acts of Literature* (New York: Routledge, 1991), 253–309.

29. Jean-François Lyotard, *The Differend: The Phrases in Dispute*, trans. Georges Van Den Abbeele and Oxford. (Minneapolis: University of Minnesota Press), 13.

30. Cathy Caruth, *Unclaimed Experience* (Baltimore: Johns Hopkins University Press, 1996); *Literature in the Ashes of History* (Baltimore: Johns Hopkins University Press, 2013); and *Trauma: Explorations in Memory*, ed. Cathy Caruth (Baltimore: Johns Hopkins University Press, 1995).

31. Herman Langbein, *People in Auschwitz* (Chapel Hill: University of North Carolina Press, 2004); Ann Kaplan, *Trauma Culture: The Politics of Terror and Loss in Media and Literature* (New Brunswick: Rutgers University Press, 2005); Michael S. Roth, *Memory, Trauma and History: Essays on Living with the Past* (New York: Columbia University Press, 2012); Agi Rubin and Henry Greenspan, in *Reflections: Auschwitz, Memory, and a Life Recreated* (Saint Paul: Paragon House, 2006); and Simone Gigliotti, *The Train Journey: Transit, Captivity, and Witnessing the Holocaust* (New York: Berghahn, 2009).

32. Dori Laub, "An Event Without a Witness: Truth, Testimony and Survival," *Testimony: Crisis of Witnessing in Literature, Psychoanalysis, and History*, ed. Shoshana Felman and Dori Laub (New York and London: Routledge, 1992).

33. See James Hatley, *Suffering Witness: The Quandary of Responsibility after the Irreparable* (Albany: State University of New York Press, 2000) and Henry W. Pickford, *The Sense of Semblance: Philosophical Analyses of Holocaust Art* (Albany: State University of New York Press, 2013).

34. Sarah R. Horowitz, *Voicing the Void: Muteness and Memory in Holocaust Fiction* (Albany: State University of New York Press, 1997).

35. R. Clifton Spargo, *Vigilant Memory: Emmanuel Levinas, the Holocaust, and the Unjust Death*. (Baltimore: Johns Hopkins University, 2006); *After Representation? The Holocaust, Literature and Culture*, ed. R. Clifton Spargo and Robert M. Ehrenreich (New Brunswick: Rutgers University Press, 2010).

36. Myra Goldenberg and Amy Shapiro, *Different Horrors, Same Hell* (Seattle and London: University of Washington Press, 2013).

37. See Zoë Waxner, *Writing the Holocaust: Identity, Testimony, Representation* (New York: Oxford University Press, 2006); David Patterson, *Wrestling with the Angel: Toward a Jewish Understanding of the Nazi Assault on the Name* (Saint Paul: Paragon House, 2006); Sarah R. Horowitz, *Voicing the Void: Muteness and Memory in Holocaust* (Albany: State University of New York Press, 1997); Marion A. Kaplan and Deborah Dash Moore, ed., *Gender and Jewish History* (Bloomington: Indiana University Press, 2011), Susan R. Suleiman, ed., *The Female Body in Western Culture: Contemporary Perspectives*, (Cambridge, MA: Harvard University Press, 1986).

38. Dan Pagis, *Points of Departure*, trans. Stephen Mitchell, introd. Robert Alter (Berkeley and Los Angeles: University of California Press, 1989).

39. Sidra DeKoven Ezrahi, *Booking Passage: Exile and Homecoming in the Modern Jewish Imagination*. Berkeley, Los Angeles, and London: University of California Press, 2000). See also Sidra DeKoven Ezrahi *By Words Alone: The Holocaust in Literature* (Chicago: University of Chicago Press, 1982).

40. Paul Celan, "Der Meridian: Rede anlässlich der Verleihung des Georg-Büchner-Preises Darmstadt, am 22. Oktober 1960," in *Gesammelte Werke in sieben Bänden* (Frankfurt: Suhrkamp Taschenbuch Verlag, 2000), 187–202.

41. Paul Celan, "Sprich auch Du," *Gesammelte Werke in sieben Bänden* (Frankfurt: Suhrkamp Taschenbuch Verlag, 2000), I, 135; "Speak You Too," in *Selected Poems and Prose of Paul Celan*, trans. John Felstiner (New York and London: W. W. Norton, 2001). See also Jerry Glenn, *Paul Celan* (New York: Twayne Publishers, 1973), 77.

42. Stéphane Moses, "Poetry after Auschwitz," in *A New History of German Literature*, ed. David E. Wellbery and Judith Ryan (Cambridge, MA: Belknap Press of Harvard University Press, 2004), 856–61.

43. Charlotte Delbo, *Auschwitz and After*, trans. Rosette C. Lamont, introd. Lawrence Langer (New Haven and London: Yale University Press, 1995).

44. Olga Lengyel, *Five Chimneys: A Woman Survivor's True Story of Auschwitz* (Chicago: Academy Chicago Publishers, 1995).

# ONE

## A Mother's Testimony as a Dwelling Place

### Dan Pagis

From the mid-1930s through 1944 the Nazi regime engaged in the systematic mass murder of European Jews. This concerted effort to annihilate six million innocent people occurred as a result of the Wannsee Conference. On January 20, 1942, fifteen high-ranking members of the Nazi party and the German government met in the southwesternmost section of Berlin, Wannsee, to coordinate the implementation of "The Final Solution of the Jewish Question." German state officials organized the deportation of Jews from throughout Europe to extermination camps in Eastern Europe. Testimonies of victims who survived the incarceration attest to the inhuman conditions inside the sealed railroad cars. Historians who describe the extreme experiences of these prisoners identify a methodical exposure to torture, dehumanization, and brutal death before arriving at the killing centers.[1]

Within the literary tradition of contemporary Hebrew poetry written in the aftermath of the Shoah, Israeli poet Dan Pagis provides one of the most touching poems in all of Holocaust literature that contextualizes the Jewish suffering during the final solution. In "Katuv b'iparon bakaron hehatum" ("Written in Pencil in the Sealed Railway-Car"), he takes up the theme of transit and places the betrayal on humankind. This poem implicitly signifies what it means to remember the undeniable suffering of innocent victims instead of relapsing into silence in the wake of the victims' death.[2] The poem appears under the section *Testimony* in Pagis's volume of poetry titled *Gilgul*, one of three volumes in his *Metamorphoses* work.[3] In the Jewish poetry series *Points of Departure,* six of Pagis's Hebrew verses appeared in English translation by Stephen Mitchell.[4]

In this short poem, Eve, the major character, elicits the urgency of recording the events by writing a message carved into the wood of the sealed railway car. At the heart of this six-line long fictive poem lies the eyewitness's appeal: addressing another witness in the cattle car to tell her son Cain about his mother and brother's deportation to the death camps. Commenting on "Katuv b'iparon," John Felstiner notes: "The briefest, tersest poem in *Gilgul* disposes nineteen words over six lines, testing with utmost quietness the limits of lyric speech *nach Auschwitz,* and testing how speech already so reduced may translate it all."[5] As Felstiner tells us, Pagis's poem, as the most stringent, strict poem in *Gilgul,* has nineteen words in six lines. It moves almost silently toward the thresholds of the lyrically speakable after Auschwitz, probing how language, already so reduced, can express what must become conscious.

> *Written in Pencil in the Sealed Railway-Car*
>> here in this carload
>> i am eve
>>
>> with abel my son
>> if you see my other son [older]
>> cain son of man [son of ben adam]
>> tell him that I [6]

Pagis' biography (1930–1986) is one of loss, suffering, and poetic testimony. He was born in Radautz near Czernowitz, Bukovina, in Romania. The language of his youth was German.[7] Most scholarly works point to the sudden separation of his family due to the father's emigration to Palestine in 1934 and his mother's death shortly after his father's departure. At the age of eleven, Pagis was deported to a concentration camp in Transnistria, Ukraine, where he spent three years of his early adolescence.[8] After surviving the camp, he arrived in 1946 in Palestine where he was reunited with his estranged father. Later, he became a schoolteacher on a Kibbutz until he moved to Jerusalem. He earned his PhD from the Hebrew University of Jerusalem where he also taught as a professor of medieval Hebrew literature. At the time of his death in 1986 in Jerusalem, he was considered to be one of the most influential Israeli poets.[9]

### THE RETELLING OF COMMITTED CRIMES

"Written in Pencil in the Sealed Railway-Car," considered to be one of the shortest lyrics in Modern Hebrew, alludes to the deportation of Jewish victims to a concentration camp.[10] Trapped within the enclosed space of a cattle car, the poem draws attention to the victims' transit. More particularly, the narrative briefly informs us about the fictional characters and the event that is happening. Eve's narrative voice identifies itself as an imprisoned inmate in a locked boxcar with her son Abel: "i am eve with abel my son." Eve's appeal to another human being is bound to the absence of Cain inside: "if you see my other son [older] cain son of man [son of ben adam]." Eve's written message ends abruptly—"*tell him that I*"—suggesting that she is unable to complete her message. Words still to be written break up after her self-referential appeal.

This poem demonstrates how the creation of a narrative involves the mode of telling and what cannot be told. Eve's role as a victim and mother can be better understood through a closer examination of her written testimony. Eve's personal story—as reflected in her written appeal—seeks another's commitment to remember the Holocaust. The insistent questions raised in the poetic text are threefold: Who is Cain's character and why is he outside of the cattle car? How do we understand Eve's role as a Jewish mother in search of her son? What ties Eve's open-ended sentence to the addressee? To answer these questions, one must determine how the investment of a possible addressee establishes the precondition of carrying Eve's story into a probable future. Looking specifically at the thematic connection of Eve's biblical name in relation to life, I argue that Eve's maternal voice functions as a mark of the feminine manifestation in Jewish thought. I will first discuss the radical rupture of Eve's voice in terms of silence, and then explore Eve's appeal through the dialogic "I/you" relationship in keeping the memory of the Holocaust alive.

As Eve's testimony shows, her invocation to an anonymous "you" opens with a conditional "if" clause that is bound up with an imminent future. Her motivation for writing aims at the fulfillment of a given condition. For example, if the "you" as addressee sees Cain, then Cain will at least get to know about his mother's effort to tell him about her persecution. Eve's gesture gives rise to a belated witnessing in the aftermath of her deportation to death. Not knowing that her voice would fail, Eve's written message is asking for the solidarity of others to carry on the message for her son.

In his book *The Belated Witness*: *Literature, Testimony and the Question of Holocaust Survival,* Michael G. Levine discusses the relation between "The Witness to The Witness" based upon Dori Laub's experience as a child survivor, analyst, and co-founder of the Fortunoff Video Archive for Holocaust Testimony. Levine notes that Laub's assessment of the belated witness is linked to the *transaction* of witnessing. A belated narrative of knowing is constructed through the witness's act of listening to the survivor's silence (the story that they are unable to recount due to the trauma they experienced firsthand) and the *independent* translation of the event that the witness derives from the untold story.[11] Eve's testimonial address unfolds as a testimony left by a eyewitness who did not survive the catastrophic event, consequently calling individual readers to become a first-person "belated witness" in the wake of the genocide.

Pagis interweaves his poetic testimony with the biblical characters of Eve and her two sons, Cain and Abel, projecting them into the history of the Holocaust. In the Genesis narrative (Genesis 4:1–16) Cain murders his brother Abel. Yet, Pagis's Eve, sealed in the railway car, has to bear the victimization along with Abel while her son Cain is absent, *outside* the railway car. There occurs an immediate resonance of remembrance: remembering the first family on earth, the first children, the first brothers, and the first violent death. In eliciting memories of the first murder, however, the poetic narrative contrasts with the biblical story. The multiplicity of Holocaust murderers, for example, does not coincide with the individual murder in the story of Cain and Abel. In Genesis, Cain's act of murder happens without Eve's presence. In contrast, in the story of the sealed railway car, Eve and Abel are annihilated together as victims of the Nazis. Both stories emerge out of the possibility of human violence and both call to mind the abusive power of the perpetrator to humiliate the victim. In his poem, Pagis deploys a plot device that draws attention to the female character of Eve in the role of both victim and mother. Furthermore, Eve's role as witness is a central concern, one which ensures the generational bearing of witness so that the memory of the Nazi crime will stay alive.

Scholars of modern Jewish poetics draw particular attention to the survivor-poet's "poetics of displacement." In her book *Booking Passage*, Sidra DeKoven Ezrahi, claims, "At home in the language and its literary genealogy, Pagis buries his own displacement deep in the cultural matrix, in the collective resonances of the language of martyrdom" (Ezrahi, 163).[12] Reading Pagis's work through the lens of displacement, Ezrahi argues that Pagis uses a language "that unmoors words from any determinate situation or fixed time and place."[13] It seems as if Pagis uses the biblical names so that Eve, Abel, and Cain can become archetypal people. Referring to this "poetics of displacement," Robert Alter notes: "If displacement has been one of the basic conditions of his own existence, the decision to make that condition into poetry was converting it from a fate passively suffered into an imaginative ordering actively achieved."[14]

Scholars observe other themes in Pagis's work as well. Ranen Omer-Sherman states that "Pagis's poetry denies the consolation of conventional narratives of finding security after catastrophe, not least in its radical unease over any safe definition of homeland."[15] In "Transformations: Holocaust Poems in Dan Pagis's *Gilgul*," Naomi Sokoloff argues for the transformative power of his artistic language claiming that his aesthetic expression of the external experience of the Nazi crime "has its own beauty or appeal in its power to signify and to make us think."[16] As these Hebrew scholars note, Pagis transmits his experiences as literature, preserving the history of the catastrophic event within a particular biblical and cultural context. Pagis as a survivor of the camps and as an artist creates an imaginary world to ensure the displacement of an untellable experience into figurative language that permits its telling.

## Inscription: A Way of Remembering

The title, *Written in Pencil in the Sealed Railway-Car*, clearly alludes to the Jewish history during Nazi Germany and underscores the significance of this form of Holocaust testimony. Pagis crosses the boundaries between artistic and historical representation in providing visual evidence of the Nazi atrocities. The title captures the specificity of deportation and of a victim's inscription that survives the Shoah as a testimonial artifact. In embodying both present and past in the title, Pagis opens a space to bear witness. The survivor-poet invites us to step inside the cattle car to read Eve's testimony, which in turn allows us to approach the unknowable — what it must have been like for the victims of the genocide.

Penciled on the wood during the journey to the extermination camps, the centrality of the title alludes to the German assault on their victims. The perfect tense of the verb "to write"—"written"—foreshadows the retelling of the historical present from within a stifling, fetid cattle car. Instead of the immediate present—"I am writing this"—the verb looks forward to a time when the writing is witnessed by others, signifying the first-hand eyewitness's yearning to create a publicly visible space for the time after the victims' death and for a shift in location, the movement between the *inside* and the *outside*. By providing a written note, Eve's eyewitness account constitutes a site of remembrance that engages others in the memory of the monstrous event of deportation inside a sealed railway car.

The word "written" tellingly designates an alternative to speaking, because speaking to another has become impossible. Being inside an enclosed space marks the impossibility of telling the event to a "Thou" outside.[17] The problem of giving oral testimony to another as exemplified in Eve's written appeal underscores the role of writing as the vehicle of transportation. The power of language as agency refers primarily to the act of testimony. At the same time, the victim's act of bearing witness establishes a relation between the victim and a possible reader within the context of Eve's writing. On the basis of the Latin root "inscribere" of the verb "to inscribe," prevails the act of writing on or in anything, from *in-* + scribere "to write." In commenting on the aesthetic form of the poet's work, Karl A. Plank draws attention to the inscribed text as artifact when he argues: "She [Eve] writes her lines within and likely on the walls of the sealed chamber, an act that endures her text as an artifact of the boxcar."[18] Looking at the text as artifact, Plank points to the relation between material culture and text.[19] The significance of testimonial writing resides in the fact that it was written by a firsthand witness in a space without escape who was condemned to death.[20]

THE SPACE OF EXPERIENCE

The opening lines of the poem, "here in this carload / I am eve / with abel my son" capture the theme of deportation. Eve begins her testimony by identifying the place of incarceration and tells us that she and her son Abel are inside a railroad car. In using the adverb "here," Pagis marks a particular moment in time, that is, the current locus of Eve's presence inside the cattle car. The expression "in this carload" plays a significant role in the narrative. The demonstrative word "this" implies that there is not only one carload but also others. In the range of transportation vehicles, the compound-noun "carload," evokes the image of a container that is filled with a large quantity of things to be carried to a specific destination. In declaring her present situation, Eve's announcement attests to the "shipment" of humans as if they were animals or inanimate things to be transported for slaughter or delivery. In his use of the term "in this carload," Pagis addresses the theme of dehumanization, remembering the Nazi's objectification of the victims in the process of their annihilation. Eve's testimonial words "here in this carload," uphold the experience of all victims who have been stripped of any right to exist as human beings.

THE BREAKING OF EVE'S VOICE

Pagis constructs Eve's task of "writing" with a radical rupture. As seen earlier, Eve, as the mother of Cain, is concerned with his presence somewhere outside the cattle car, where he remains ignorant of what happened to his mother. The narrative content focuses on Eve's appeal to others to tell her son something—perhaps what has happened to her and to Abel—but Pagis situates Eve's imperative within a fragmentary mode of writing. Eve's effort to complete her sentence fails: "tell him that I." Focusing on "fragmentary exigency in Holocaust literature," Dorota Glowacka writes: "The paradoxical power of the fragment lies not only in its centrifugal unframing of the narrative content but also in its ability to release the power of the untold in the spaces between the scraps of memory."[21] The rhetorical figure of *aposiopesis*, or the act of falling silent, is typically used to bring the auditor's imagination into play—"to release the power of the untold."[22] The enigmatic history of Eve's "falling voice," I suggest, is embedded within the future response of the addressee.[23] It is the abrupt silence of the "I," the breaking of Eve's voice that juxtaposes both the indirect mode of reference and the structure of displacement on the part of Eve's elliptical writing. Despite Eve's plea to someone outside, the nameless addressee lacks her precise message of what to tell her son.

This lack resides in the speaker's breaking voice, possibly evoked through Eve's death inside the car or after her arrival in the extermination camps.

## A MOTHER'S CALL TO ANOTHER

In the narrative, Pagis bridges the gap between knowing and unknowing by creating a metonymic relation between the speaker and the addressee. As the text shows, the addressee and Cain are outside the cattle car. Entrapped in a locked space, Eve writes: *"if you see my other son [older], tell him."* Notably, rather than addressing her son Cain directly, Eve is asking another to tell him. Uncannily, the poet's choice of pronouns builds a direct relationship between the "I" and the "you." Pagis frames the unfolding event between Eve and a poetic apostrophe without any indication that Eve's distinct message reaches anyone. In her book titled *Talk Fiction: Literature and the Talk Explosion*, Irene Kacandes investigates the literary relationship between the *"I/You"* through the works of the philosopher Martin Buber, the literary critic Barbara Johnson, and the linguist Émile Benveniste to develop her concept of the "narrative apostrophe."[24] She proclaims that "talk of narrative apostrophe" is constituted "by vocative force and the fiction on which it rests."[25] Arguing that a first-person narrator tells a story primarily through addressing a "you" character who does not reply, Kacandes proposes that the second person pronoun "you" is the "preeminent sign of interaction."[26] By foregrounding the first-person's vocative force of animating a "you" to respond, she argues that texts written in this apostrophic mode of narration "constitute an obvious if complex form of talk fiction, since orientation toward exchange (Talk) is always based on a fiction: that the 'you' is animate and capable of response (whereas the 'you' is actually absent, dead or inanimate)."[27] For her, "a specific actual reader is being called by the narrating voice in the text, whereas any reader could feel called by it."[28] What is of utmost importance in Kacandes's concept is that a reader's reply involves not so much the proper attitude of listening as the recognition that one is called both to identify and not to identify with the "you." According to her, in a *narrative apostrophe*, the speaker addresses someone who is (seemingly) being addressed to provoke response in someone else. Kacandes associates the term of "Talk of apostrophe" with "performance" rather than actual "dialogue," to highlight the active role of readers. Therefore, the occurrence of Eve's address to a "you" is linked to a performative act.

Remember that Eve's address "tell him" is twofold. It signifies not only her desperation for a response to her testimony after her death but also her desire to let Cain know about her fate. While the latter reveals her maternal concern, the former indicates a continuation of collective remembrance. Regarding Eve's address, I wish to read the second-person pronoun "you" as the figure of *a transit witness*. In becoming *a transit* witness, it is necessary for a possible "you" not only to respond to Eve's inscription but also to transmit her message to another who in turn will create a discourse in response to Eve's original writing. Eve's address "tell him" signifies, I argue, not only her desperation to tell her son Cain but also to reach someone who will reply at a time after her death. The space of transit can be considered the gap between the "I," and the "you" not knowing what has happened inside while Eve was writing the letter. As discussed earlier, in addressing an absent "you," Eve empowers a possible reader to transport her story from inside the cattle car into public memory. Regarding Eve's performative act, we can recall Kacandes' argument that "apostrophe is a particularly obvious kind of talk fiction because it makes so apparent that it aims, not at dialogue, but at mediated forms of interaction." [29]

In *History in Transit*, Dominick LaCapra returns to his earlier work on trauma, and focuses on the interaction between history and historiography and history and critical theory; he especially points to the hyperbolic rhetoric of contemporary theorists associated with traumatic memories such as those of the Holocaust. [30] Arguing that history is always in motion, he writes: "History is always in transit, even if periods, places, or professions sometimes achieve relative stabilization." [31] Addressing the transhistorical nature of history and its traumatic dimension LaCapra understands the writing of history as a process of unstable and constantly changing relationships. In his study, he develops the concepts of identity and experience, in particular, as they are associated with traumatic experiences such as those of the Holocaust, and their role in a historical understanding.

The figure of the "transit witness" signifies that the nameless "you" as a possible reader is especially significant for passing on the historical testimony inside Eve's cattle car. Though reading the figure of a "transit witness" cannot be measured with the transference of a historical eyewitness, the apostrophic "you" as a *transit witness* itself yields the ethical transit between art (the literary) and history. If history writing is unstable and changing and based on relationships and current interpretations, then, the creation of a fictive transit witness is as inherently historical as it is literary, and literature IS history writing. This means, the story told from the inside to the outside will transit from one reader to another and be altered in the new you's consciousness. Passing the story from one reader to another ensures that Eve, Abel, and all other victims inside the cattle car will remain alive in the midst of their death. Emphasizing the interchange between the "I/You," Pagis displaces Eve's abrupt lapse into silence onto a responsive reader who will bear witness within language. In addressing the importance of the reader, Plank points out that the double responsibility of the reader lies in the process of hearing and transmitting Eve's silent note.[32] The goal of the addressee as the figure of "the transit witness" is to carry the inmates from the space inside to the outside, to evoke a public consciousness. If a possible "you" is attentive to Eve's plea, the possibility of transits happens through the retelling of her testimony. In other words, it is precisely the Other's language that can be seen as a vehicle to transit Eve's story into a vibrant life of remembrance. Bringing Eve's story from the "inside" and the past to the present "outside," symbolically means the opening of the enclosed space and that the victim's senseless death in the extermination camps is not the end of her story. By bringing forward Eve's plea into the present, Eve's inscription is repeatedly returning to public awareness with the potential to reach an Other who will transmit the story of the past into the present and future generations.

## In the Book of Genesis

How do we understand Pagis's choice to create Eve's fictive voice whose name is inextricably bound to the biblical catastrophe of the first family? How do we understand her maternal nature in relation to Cain? Eve of the Genesis narrative continues to be a central theme in the history of human creation and female existence. In *Rediscovering Eve: Ancient Israelite Women in Context*, Carol Meyers discusses Eve's relevance to the ancient Near Eastern World: "Not only does Eve represent Israelite women, she is also a product of the way of life of the women in that world."[33] To understand a women's way of life in ancient Israel, Meyers considers her in the context as "Everywoman Eve" arguing that the reality of ancient Israel informs the reality the biblical Eve faces when she leaves the Garden of Eden.

According to Genesis 2:22, God casts Adam into sleep and drew from him a rib, from which the first woman, Eve, was fashioned. The English name Eve is derived from the Hebrew name *Chavah*, the Hebrew root of which is "life." And we are told in Genesis 3:20 that Adam would name his wife Eve because she would become the mother of all life. The literary role of Eve as a mother is rooted in the biblical tale in which she has to endure the killing of her son Abel [הֶבֶל][ הֶבֶל, Hevel] by his brother Cain [קַיִן, Qayin]. How do we understand Pagis's choice to create Eve's fictive voice whose name is inextricably bound to the biblical catastrophe of the first family? How do we understand her maternal voice in relation to Cain?

Poetic composition is inextricably linked to the biblical name of Eve, the mother of Cain and Abel. Eve's Hebrew name "*Chavah*," is a derivative of the Hebrew word *chayah*, meaning "living one." The root of this name is connected with the word Chaya which means living, and the word "Chai" which means life. "Chava" is in causative form—that is, she caused all the people in the future to live ("Rashi" Genesis 3:20 with

"Siftei Chachamim"). In the Torah, Eve is *em kol chai*—the mother of all life (Genesis 3:20). Chavah embodies both the essence of life itself and the creative ability to grant that life to others. As with most of the names in the Torah, the Torah explains the significance of this name, which was given to her by Adam: "The man called his wife's name Chava, because she had become the mother of all the living" (Genesis 3:20). The idea of "mother of all life" expresses not only the ability to physically give birth, but also to create, nourish, and enhance all facets of life. Therefore, Chavah is not only the mother of life but also represents the experience of life.[34] Linking the Hebrew name "Chavah" to Eve's motherhood in the story of transportation provides a larger context for the notion of duality in relation to Eve as the archetype of mother. In order to examine the notion of the mother, a reading of the figure of Eve as a mother becomes irresistible. How can we understand Eve's role in the search for her son Cain?

## A MOTHER'S NARRATIVE POWER

In contrast to Meyer's analysis of Eve as an ordinary woman of ancient Israel, David Patterson sheds light on how to read and understand Eve as the first biblical woman and her prominent role as a female figure in Jewish teachings. Given the Nazi's plan to destroy European Jews, murderous actions against pregnant Jewish women and childbirth aimed in particular at the annihilation of all Jewish life. In his article, "The Nazi Assault on the Jewish Soul through the Murder of the Jewish Mother," Patterson reorients, I suggest, our understanding of the feminine presence in all of Jewish life.[35] He addresses the murder of the Jewish mother through theological aspects in a Jewish religious life arguing that the Nazi's anti-Semitism was based "upon a *metaphysical* difference." According to Patterson, Judaism was blamed for having a different view of G-d, the world, and humanity: "If the Nazis are to be Nazis, then they *have to* eliminate the notion of a higher, divine image within the human being that places upon each of us an infinite responsibility for the *other* human being."[36]

Patterson's statement that the source of the Jewish soul is the Jewish mother hints at the relation between the Jewish mother and the feminine in the Jewish tradition. According to Jewish teaching, "woman" is not only the "Other" beyond all ontological categories, "she opens up the very otherness of the interrelation that defines humanity, as well as the mystery of divinity, as a giving, over and against conquering." To understand the central role of women Patterson attempts to retrieve the figure of the feminine in the mystical teachings of the Zohar. In the kabbalistic text, *Shekhinah* defines the feminine manifestation of the Holy One. The concept of the *Shekhinah* considers woman to be a part of God, not a separate deity. Moreover, the primary kabbalistic text is used to describe that the feminine enters the world through the marriage between G-d and Israel, between husband and wife. According to the Zohar, the foundation of a home is not a man but a necessary woman and with the presence of the feminine knowing that Shekhinah departs not from the house or from the world.[37]

FEMININE MANIFESTATION AND DWELLING

What is inextricably linked to the feminine presence of the Holy One is the creation of a dwelling place in the world. In Jewish teaching, the possibility for "home" or "dwelling place" is tied to the first letter of the Torah, the letter beit. Patterson explains that the commandment of the Torah lies not in being obedient but in the act of transforming the world into a dwelling place for something—or for someone holy: "Indeed, the meaning of the Torah is given in the first letter of Torah, in the beit, which also means home or dwelling place for holiness, and that task is accomplished most fundamentally through the feminine."[38]

Thus, the woman is the feminine manifestation of the Holy One is indebted with the primary responsibility of transforming the world into a dwelling place. Given the pivotal significance of *home* in Jewish thought, Patterson comments on the Nazi's determination to make "the Jews *homeless* before they murdered them: living in a camp, a ghetto, or in hiding, *every Jew was homeless*. This homelessness is the manifestation of the Nazi assault on the feminine, which is an assault on the *beit*—on the home—that is the origin and essence of the Torah."[39]

In addition, Patterson explains the significance of the Jewish mother in relation to be recognized as a Jew in Jewish tradition:

> According to Jewish tradition, to have an origin—to have a mother—is to be already marked for a mission: origin implies destiny, when that origin is seen as a *mother* and not as some primeval ooze. Situated at the origin of human sanctity, the mother represents not the primeval but the immemorial, the remembrance of something that transforms everything, prior to everything, and forever afterward into something *meaningful*. Therefore, it is a Jewish mother, and not a Jewish father, that makes a Jew a Jew.[40]

As evidenced, the complexity of the Jewish mother representing the immemorial can ultimately transform everything into something meaningful. It is this significance of the Jewish mother and her "feminine manifestation" (ability), I argue, to create a dwelling place, that is at work in the figure of Eve as a mother remembering and calling upon her son at the moment of death.

A Feminine Response of Giving

In using the biblical names of Eve, Cain, and Abel, (sons of Adam), Pagis alludes to the archaic fratricide in mythic history. In the book of Genesis, the rejection of Cain's sacrifice initiates the motivation for his violent act of murder.[41] In the biblical text of Cain and Abel, Eve has to bear the burden of being the mother of a murdered child and of a murderer. In the narrative of the *Sealed Railway-Car*, the mother figure of Eve returns, telling a story in which the history of murder repeats itself, this time not as individual but as mass murder. In the catastrophic event of the deportation, Eve declares herself and Adam to be victims, acknowledging that her firstborn son Cain is not inside the car. Eve's narrative text provides no reference for Cain's uncanny disappearance. Although Cain is not explicitly identified as a Nazi perpetrator, his name resonates with the figure of the fraternal murderer. Recalling Cain's act of murder in the book of Genesis, how do we understand Eve's search for her oldest son as she asks others to "tell" him about their victimization through an addressee? Eve's appeal serves as an allegory for maternal love emanating as responsibility for the other.

In his essay "The Holocaust and the Economy of Memory from Bellow to Morrison (The Technique of Figurative Allegory)," R. Clifton Spargo explores the notion of figurative allegory, referring to the term as a rhetorical procedure depending on the transpositional properties of metaphoric exchange.[42] For him, "Allegory is historicizing, even rehistoricizing; and by this alternate emphasis it may develop, as a textually generative principle, imperatives returning us not only to the literality of the story but also to much of its invoked historical context."[43] Following Spargo's framework, Pagis transposes the story of Cain and Abel into a figurative allegory promoting two levels of reference in which, as Spargo suggests, first-order reference yields to second order reference. In so doing, Eve's testimonial note intrinsically alludes to the murderer by reminding us of the biblical story.

The question to be raised is Eve's remembrance of Cain in the moment of her own death. Spargo emphasizes Eve's ethics of memory, arguing that she, in the anticipation of her death, still remembers her murderous son.[44] For him, the poem's absence of punctuation underlies the reader's possibility of completing Eve's thoughts, "if only hypothetically, if only thereafter to undo it." For example, he makes clear that a thought such as *"tell him that I . . . forgive him"* cannot be reconciled with Judaism since this constructed thought on one hand asserts "a Christianized narrative of sacrificial suffering" and on the other hand "would redeem the mother's suffering for the good of history."[45] Bringing together Pagis's poetic testimony and Levinas's ethics of subjectivity as the responsibility for the other as seen through the figure of Eve, Spargo suggests an alternative mode of remembrance as an extension of the victim through us as readers.[46]

## A MOTHER'S CREATION OF A DWELLING PLACE

As noted, Patterson identifies three essential features that define the unique role of the Jewish mother and her feminine presence: 1) Otherness, 2) Feminine, and 3) Dwelling Place. Following Spargo's suggestion to complete Eve's thought, regarding "Eve's ethics of memory," demonstrates how Eve's maternal enactment relates to Levinas's concept of love as responsibility for the Other. First, is its importance in the context of remembering the other. Second, Eve's attempt to tell Cain what has happened to her and to Abel can be seen as a call for justice. In *Is It Righteous to Be?* Levinas takes up the notion of love as the beginning of responsibility for the other:

> The encounter with the other is straightaway my responsibility for him. That is the responsibility for my neighbor, which is no doubt the severe name for what we call love of one's neighbor: love without eros, charity, love in which the ethical aspect dominates the passionate aspect, love without concupiscence. I don't like very much the word *love*, which is worn out and debased. Let us speak instead of taking upon oneself the fate of the other.[47]

As Levinas explains, the root of ethical responsibility for the other originates from "love of one's neighbor." At the heart of Eve's appeal lies her response to human suffering and her sense of obligation toward the other. Condemned to death with all innocent victims in the *Sealed Railway-Car*, Eve's primary purpose for writing the testimonial note "*tell him that I*" affirms her concern for Cain and asserts her responsibility for the other. By revealing that she is entrapped with anonymous victims, Eve takes into account the memory of others. In other words, despite her own deportation, Eve's "ethics of memory" is linked to her love for others. In this view, Eve's selfless act, I propose, can also be linked to her feminine yearning for creating a "dwelling place" beyond her death. Patterson cites Levinas on the notion of dwelling: "The Dwelling is not a situation in the objective world, but the objective world is situated by my relation to my dwelling."[48] Reading Levinas's sentence in relation to Eve's appeal shows that she places the other at the center of her testimonial act. Her responsibility toward the other is emphasized in her appeal to make the inaccessible past "dwell" for future generations.

At the center of Eve's testimonial note lies her maternal feminine role in Jewish thought. As described by Patterson, the significance of the feminine opens up "the very otherness of the interrelation" that characterizes humanity. Thus, the interrelation between love and the responsibility for the Other, I suggest, is embedded within Eve's writing.

Let's remember the relevant relationship between woman and dwelling. In order to understand the importance of "home," Patterson argues that the Nazis systematic assault on the Jewish people was to render the Jewish people homeless: "This homelessness is a manifestation of the Nazi assault on the feminine, which is an assault on the *beit*—on the home—that is the origin and essence of the Torah."[49] Eve's invocative call to appeal to another to tell Cain, I suggest, stems from the Nazi's fatal refusal to allow Jews a home—a dwelling space that makes room for both the dweller and others. Since the creation of the home stands at the center of the feminine, Eve's address to a "you" can also be linked to her feminine task to create a dwelling place in the midst of death. Eve seems to want to transform the senseless and crucial death of others into a space in which the memory can dwell and unfold in remembrance. In his commentary on the feminine in Jewish teaching, Rabbi Yitzchack Ginsburg underscores that the womb symbolizes the purpose of making room for another rather than usurping its place: "There is no giving more profound than giving birth, no giving more profoundly holy" says the Jewish teaching.[50] This feminine activity can be linked to Eve's appeal. The root of creating a dwelling place for the manifestation of God seems to arise from Eve's responsibility for the other. What lies at the core of Eve's appeal—to use Spargo's term—is "Eve's ethic of memory." Eve's creation of a dwelling place by initiating a relationship between the dead and a possible reader who in turn reinitiates the solidarity among other individual subjects shows that she places the other before herself.

In the moment of death, Eve does not leave her life in the hands of her murderers, knowing that she would be dead. By writing a note to another, Eve obligates her life to the other, and therefore, symbolically gives birth to the survival of the Other. It is precisely her individual appeal to an unknown addressee that bears the responsibility for the Other. Eve's request makes it obvious that her concern to remember all innocent victims represents a woman in Jewish thought who most notably transforms a senseless death into a life of survival. Eve's performative act confirms the Jewish teachings that "the turning toward another is what defines the movement in the direction of home that makes dwelling possible."[51] In establishing a relationship with another, Eve's invocative act can be considered essential for creating a "dwelling place" or "a home" for all anonymous victims who have been persecuted and annihilated in a state of "homelessness."

## A Mother's Ethical Response

Faced with her death, Eve is compelled to call upon Cain who is outside the space of victimization of the cattle car. Her son's absence, reflected in her address, *"if you see my son Cain tell him that I . . ."* explains why her maternal search for him is so anguished. Pagis alludes to the first murder in human history by using Cain's name. Thus, for the reader, the figure of Cain can be seen from the perspective of a perpetrator. In his reading of the poem, Spargo suggests that Cain can be read as a figure for the Nazi themselves: "Eve implores the anonymous, hostile world for which her other son [Cain] is held largely responsible."[52] As seen earlier, at issue is Eve's concern for telling her son about her deportation. In asking an unknown other, Eve seems to ensure that Cain's name is uttered before he hears his mother's message. In describing the notion of "home" in Jewish thought, Patterson makes evident what it means to call a person's name in relation to a dwelling place: "The home, for example, is where our name is first uttered with love, announcing that we are a real, flesh-and-blood human being; this utterance of our name and not the determination of an essence tells us that we are someone whose life has meaning."[53] Since the most profound originality of creating a home is to make possible the calling of the name, Eve yearningly calling Cain's name comes from her love as a mother. In the moment of her death, she remembers her son, for his own sake. Unable to know his hand in the death of others, Eve's urgent search—or call—for Cain lies in her concern that he is "a man [who] did not see his brothers" (Exodus 10:23).[54] Let's remind ourselves that Pagis's poetic composition opens a space to hypothetically complete Eve's testimonial note. In so doing, we see that Eve is telling her son: "I utter your name, calling upon you as one of the perpetrators who has rendered our lives into something meaningless by making us not only homeless but also by murdering us." In Jewish teaching, only in doing good for another can the identity of ourselves be established. In the context of Cain's identity as a Nazi figure, it seems as if Eve as his mother repeats the question once asked by God: "What have you done" (Genesis 4:10). Therefore, Eve's search for Cain can be seen as an effort to seek him out for murderous actions in her very absence.

## A MOTHER'S LOVE — A MOTHER'S CALL FOR JUSTICE

In the perspective of the Nazi assault against Jewish mothers, the issue of ethical violence is central to Eve's search for her son. In a 1983 interview, "Philosophy, Justice and Love," Levinas reflects on Cain's answer to God when asked about his brother Abel, arguing that his response—"Am I my brother's keeper?"—exemplifies his lack of ethics. He suggests that Cain's answer shows that Cain sees himself and Abel to be rigorously separated ontological beings: "I am I, and he is he."[55] For Levinas, the ethical is defined by relationship: "The only absolute value is the human possibility of giving the other priority over oneself."[56] He explains that the relation to another emanates from my obligation to him with respect to my own relation with God: "In my relation to the other, I hear God. . . .

I am not saying that the other is God, but that in his or her face, I hear the word of God."[57] It is in this sense that Eve's appeal signifies not only a mother's love for her son but also her feminine presence. In conjunction with the thematic relation to her son and his possible murderous actions, Eve's written testimony encompasses Levinas's understanding of responsibility with respect to the other: "I am responsible for the other even when he bothers me, even when he persecutes me. . . . But I am responsible for the persecution of my neighbors. If I belong to a people, that people and my kind are all my neighbors. They have a right to defense, just as do those who are not my kin."[58]

Borrowing Spargo's suggestion that Cain represents the figure of the Nazi, Eve's attempt to call upon her son defines not only her responsibility to Cain as the Other but also to the victims, the neighbors, systematically annihilated under the Nazi genocide. The very fact that Eve wants to tell Cain "that I" attests not only to her responsibility to her son/Other as persecutor but to the Other(s) as persecuted in the cattle car. Eve's responsibility for the other, the persecutor and the persecuted, consists of an asymmetrical relation as seen in Levinas's theory on ethical responsibility: "At the outset I hardly care what the other is with respect to me, that is his.[59] Thus, I argue, Eve's individual effort to approach her son without reciprocity embodies her maternal love, reminding him of her as the one who created a home for him. Levinas explains: "This responsibility for the other is the grounding moment of love. It is not really a state of mind; it is not a sentiment, but rather an obligation."[60]

Thus, Eve's request to *tell* her son emerges out of an obligation for the Other, out of her love for her (possible murderous) son. Yet, inasmuch Eve's appeal expresses the love for her son, the creation of a dwelling place for the dead underlies her ethical responsibility for the Others beyond their death.

In his writings on justice, Levinas points out that love is originary, and commanded. As such, it signifies an ethical responsibility based on a principal of human individuation. Derived from the holy, the relation to God, Levinas notes, cannot be described without speaking of one's concern for the other.[61] With this issue in mind, Eve's individuation emerges by virtue of her being responsible for the other. Let's remember that in Jewish thought dwelling is characterized by giving, a giving that is linked to life. In the story of Eve, we have seen how her appeal to another aims at a return to a home in which the memory of others can dwell in the future. A related expression referring to the Hebrew word "return," teshuvah, is the word "response," which exemplifies Eve's response to her own deportation and to the deportations of everyone in the cattle car. Her responsibility for the other is a giving without reciprocity, solely linked to the memory of others.[62] In contrast to a justice that includes the state, Eve's appeal, in particular her calling upon Cain, manifests itself as a personal, as an individual justice. Her maternal love shows, on the one hand, in her love for her son who committed crimes, and on the other hand her written testimony attests to responsibility for the others deported to death in the cattle car. What seems to be essential based on her written testimony is that Eve's sense of justice consists in creating a dwelling place for remembering the victims who were murdered—in a sense—by her own son. In Levinas's words, "Individual justice can only be done by remembering the Other. By remembering the Other, I remind you that you were guilty of the crime."[63]

## CONCLUSION

One of the prominent features in Jewish teaching is the feminine manifestation as part of the Holy One. From a Jewish perspective, "maternal love is the manifestation of the Most High in our very midst."[64] Eve's search for Cain can be seen as an effort to call upon him for his murderous actions, revealing that her responsibility for the Other lies in the re-creating of a dwelling place as a space of remembrance. Eve's language evokes the idea in Jewish thought that woman can transform anything into something meaningful. This maternal love can be seen in a mother's appeal to her son. Eve's responsibility for Cain imposes itself as recognition of him as her son and but also as a murderer. In the relation between Eve as the mother and Cain as her son, Eve calls upon him for his own sake. The figure of Eve plays a major role in asserting judicial dependence. In terms of possible murderous acts, Cain has to be held accountable for his actions. The figure of Eve, who also represents the mother of all on this earth, calls upon Cain, whose name stands in for Nazi perpetration.

## NOTES

1. For a general overview of Nazi attitudes and policies toward Jews see Raul Hilberg, *The Destruction of the European Jews* (Chicago: Quadrangle Books, 1961); Doris Bergen, *The Holocaust: A Concise History* (Lanham, MD: 2009); Christopher Browning, *The Origin of the Final Solution. The Evolution of Nazi Jewish P.* . . .http://www.orte-der-rinnerung.de/en/institutions/institutions_liste/house_of_the_wannsee_conference_memorial_and_education.

2. Susan Gubar, *Poetry after Auschwitz: Remembering What One Never Knew* (Bloomington: Indiana University Press, 2003), 1–27. In the chapter "The Holocaust Is Dying," Susan Gubar examines the historical periods of the 1940s, 1950s, and 1960s, in which the Holocaust was fading from memory. She addresses in particular the political and scientific resistance in Europe to engage with the causes and ramifications of the Holocaust, the lack of memory, and the denial of the Shoah. In addition, she points to the works of literary representations of the Holocaust and advocates poetry as the form that provides vision, truthful and baffling pictures "flashing up at the instant when it [i.e., the truth of what happened] can be recognized and is never seen again." This is in direct contrast to Theodor Adorno's famous statement, 1949, that "to write poetry after Auschwitz is barbaric."

3. Dan Pagis, *Gilgul* (Tel Aviv: Massada, 1970).

4. Dan Pagis, *Point of Departure*, trans. Stephen Mitchell, introd. Robert Alter (Philadelphia: The Jewish Publication Society of America, 1982).

5. John Felstiner, "The *Gilgul* of Dan Pagis: Myth, History, Silence," *Translation Review* 32–33, no.1 (1990): 8.

6. Dan Pagis, *Point of Departure*, 23. "Katuv b'iparon bakaron hehatum" (Written in Pencil in the Sealed Railway-Car), *Gilgul* (Ramat Gan: Massada, 1970), 22. The poem was originally published in Hebrew by Massada, 1970.

7. See the article by Amir Eshel and Thomas Sparr, "Zur Topographie der Herkunft in der Lyrik von Dan Pagis and Paul Celan," *Special Issue of Jewish Studies* 18.3. (Spring 2013): 115–28. The article compares the biographical information with the essential points of their poetic works.

8. Sidra DeKoven Ezrahi, "Reclaiming a Plot in Radautz. Dan Pagis and the Prosaics of Memory," in *Booking Passage: Exile and Homecoming in the Modern Jewish Imagination* (Berkeley and Los Angeles: University of California Press, 2000), 157.

9. Ranen Omer-Sherman, "Responding to the Burden of Witness in Dan Pagis's 'Written in Pencil in the Sealed Railway-Car'," *Teaching the Representation of the Holocaust*, ed. Marianne Hirsch and Irene Kacandes (New York: The Modern Language Association of America, 2004), 303–14.

10. Ranen Omer-Sherman, 311.

11. Michael G. Levine, *The Belated Witness: Literature, Testimony, and the Question of Holocaust Survival* (Stanford: Stanford University Press, 2006) 5, 5n14, 191. See also Shoshana Felman and Dori Laub, *Testimony: Crises of Witnessing in Literature, Psychoanalysis, and History* (New York and London: Routledge, 1992).

12. Sidra DeKoven Ezrahi, *Booking Passage, Exile and Homecoming in the Modern Jewish Imagination* (Berkeley, Los Angeles, London: University of California Press, 2000).

13. Sidra DeKoven Ezrahi, "Dan Pagis and the Poetics of Incoherence," in *Remembering for the Future Working Papers and Addenda*, ed. Yehuda Bauer et al (New York: Pergamon Press, 1989), 2418.

14. Dan Pagis, *Points of Departure*, Jewish poetry series, trans. Stephen Mitchell, introd. Robert Alter (Philadelphia: Jewish Publication Society of America, 5742/1981) xiii, xv. In the poems that deal directly with genocide, this use of distanced and multiple voices is linked with an impulse to pull apart the basic categories of existence and reassemble them in strange configurations that expose the full depth of the outrage perpetrated.

15. Ranen Omer-Sherman, "Cross-Currents," *Association for Religion and Intellectual Life* 54, no. 2 (Summer 2004): 51–60.

16. Naomi Sokoloff, "Transformations: Holocaust Poems in Dan Pagis's *Gilgul*," *Hebrew Annual Review* 8 (1984): 217.

17. Dori Laub, "An Event Without a Witness: Truth, Testimony and Survival," in Shoshana Felman and Dori Laub, *Testimony: Crises of Witnessing in Literature, Psychoanalysis, and History* (New York and London: Routledge, 1992), 81–82. Dori Laub, a child survivor and cofounder of the Fortunoff Video Archive for Holocaust Testimonies at Yale, discusses in this chapter the notion of a witness from inside. According to him, at moments such as this, there was "no longer an other to which one could say 'Thou' in the hope of being heard or recognized as a subject, of being heard. . . . One could not bear witness to oneself."

18. Karl. A. Plank, *Mother of the Wire Fence: Inside and Outside the Holocaust* (Louisville: Westminster John Knox Press), 47.

19. Elaine Scarry, *The Body in Pain: The Making and Unmaking of the World* (New York and Oxford: Oxford University Press, 1987), 318–19. Scarry defines an artifact as an object that requires "sustained imagining."

20. Jennifer Hansen-Glucklich, "Disfigured Memory: The Reshaping of Holocaust Symbols in Yad Vashem and the Jewish Museum in Berlin," in *Nexus: Essays in German Jewish Studies*, ed. William C. Donahue and Martha Helfer (Rochester: Camden House, 2011), 211, 218. Dan Pagis's famous poem, "Written in Pencil in the Sealed Railway-Car," can be read on the railway car of the Memorial to the Deportees overlooking the

hills of Jerusalem. Moshe Safdie, the architect of the New Yad Vashem Holocaust History Memorial, inscribed the poem on the viewing platform to echo the memory of a railway station.

21. Dorota Glowacka, "The Scattered Word: Writing of the Fragment and Holocaust Testimony," in *The Holocaust's Ghost: Writing on Art, Politics, Law and Education*, ed. F.C. DeCoste and Bernhard Schwartz, (Edmonton: University of Alberta Press, 2000), 37.

22. "Aposiopesis," Encyclopaedia Britannica Online Academic Edition. Encyclopaedia Britannica Inc., 2014, accessed July 15, 2014. http://www.britannica.com/EB checked/topic/30202/aposiopesis.

23. Cathy Caruth, *Unclaimed Experience: Trauma, Narrative and History* (Baltimore: John Hopkins University Press, 1996), 89–90. Caruth draws attention to the rhetoric of falling in light of Paul de Man's "The Resistance to Theory," in *Modern Criticism and Theory, A Reader*, ed. David Lodge and Nigel Woods (London and New York: Routledge, 1988). In her study of trauma in literature, Caruth claims that the figure of falling registers as an indirect mode of reference.

24. Irene Kacandes, *Talk Fiction: Literature and the Talk Explosion* (Lincoln: University of Nebraska Press, 2001), 149. Buber describes the relationship between the "I" and the "you" as follows: "When I get out of 'myself' in order to establish a living relationship with a being, of necessity I encounter or I post a 'you,' who is the only imaginable 'person' outside of me," 191, 201.

25. Kacandes, 145.

26. Ibid.

27. Ibid.

28. Ibid.

29. Ibid., 155.

30. Sara Guyer, "Remembering, Repeating . . . Review of Amy Hungerford, *The Holocaust of Texts, Genocide, Literature, and Personification* and Dominick LaCapra, *History in Transit: Experience, Identity, Critical Theory*," *Contemporary Literature* 46, no. 4 (Winter 2005): 736–45.

31. Dominick LaCapra, *History in Transit: Experience, Identity, Critical Theory* (Ithaca and London: Cornell University Press), 1.

32. Karl A. Plank, *Mother of the Wire Fence: Inside and Outside the Holocaust* (Louisville: Westminster John Knox Press, 1994), 49.

33. Carol Meyers, *Rediscovering Eve: Ancient Israelite Women in Context* (New York: Oxford University Press, 2013), 2.

34. The question though still remains as to why Chavah wasn't called Chayah? What is the difference between these two names? When looking at them in their Hebrew spelling, the difference in each name is one letter. The name Chavah has a *vav* which is numerically equal to six, and Chaya has the letter *yud* which is numerically equal to 10. The difference between these two numbers is four, the letter *dalet*. Rabbi Ginsburgh teaches that if we add the letter *dalet* to the name Chavah, we get the word *chedvah*, meaning "joy." This teaches us that we transform Chavah into Chayah, into "life," when she can birth with joy. The second understanding of the name Chavah focuses on its connection to the word *chavayah*, which means experience. Chavah is not only the mother of life but also represents the experience of life. http://www.chabad. org/theJewishWoman/article_cdo/aid/335943/jewish/Chav/Mother-of-All-Life.ht.

35. David Patterson, "The Nazi Assault on the Jewish Soul through the Murder of the Jewish Mother," in *Different Horrors. Same Hell: Gender and the Holocaust*, ed. Myrna Goldenberg and Amy Shapiro (Seattle: University of Washington Press, 2013), 169–76.

36. Ibid., 164.

37. David Patterson, *Hebrew Language, Jewish Thought* (New York: Taylor & Francis, 2004), 145.

38. Ibid., 165–66.

39. Patterson, "The Nazi Assault on the Jewish Soul," 166.

40. Ibid., 166–67.

41. R. Clifton Spargo, *Vigilant Memory: Emmanuel Levinas, the Holocaust, and the Unjust Death* (Baltimore: Johns Hopkins University Press, 2006), 101–05. Spargo reads Cain's reply to God, "Am I my brother's keeper," as a nonanswer, arguing that his reply to God epitomizes the Levinasian connotation of bad conscience. In addition, Spargo discusses diverse interpretations of the Hebrew text regarding the gap (Cain's missing intention to kill his brother) between the rejection of Cain's sacrifice and the act of murder.

42. R. Clifton Spargo, "The Holocaust and the Economy of Memory from Bellow to Morrison: The Technique of Figurative Allegory," in *After Representation? The Holocaust, Literature and Culture,* ed. R. Clifton Spargo and Robert M. Ehrenreich, (New Brunswick: Rutgers University Press in association with the United States Holocaust Memorial Museum, 2010), 137–78.

43. Ibid., 153–54.

44. Cliff Spargo, *Vigilant Memory. Emmanuel Levinas, the Holocaust, and the Unjust Death,* (Baltimore: Johns Hopkins University Press, 2006), 177.

45. Ibid., 177.

46. Ibid., 177–78.

47. Jill Robbins, ed., *Is It Righteous to Be? Interviews with Emmanuel Levinas* (Stanford: Stanford University Press, 2001), 165.

48. David Patterson, *Genocide in Jewish Thought* (New York: Oxford University Press, 2012), 172.

49. Ibid., 166.

50. Ibid., 166.

51. Ibid., 173.

52. Spargo, *Vigilant Memory,* 177.

53. Patterson, *Genocide,* 172.

54. Ibid., 56.

55. Robbins, *Is It Righteous,* 171–72.

56. Ibid., 170.

57. Ibid., 171.

58. Ibid., 177.

59. Ibid., 166.

60. Ibid., 166.

61. Ibid., 171.

62. Patterson, *Genocide,* 173.

63. Robbins, 166.

64. Ibid., 168.

# TWO

## Remembrance of the M/other/tongue

### Paul Celan

*SPRICH AUCH DU*

*Sprich auch du,*
*sprich als letzter,*
*sag deinen Spruch.*
*Sprich —*
*Doch scheide das Nein nicht vom Ja.*
*Gib deinem Spruch auch den Sinn:*
*gib ihm den Schatten.*
*Gib ihm Schatten genug,*
*gib ihm so viel,*
*als du um dich verteilt weißt zwischen*
*Mittnacht und Mittag und Mittnacht.*
*Blicke umher:*
*sieh, wie's lebendig wird rings —*
*Beim Tode! Lebendig!*
*Wahr spricht, wer Schatten spricht.*
*Nun aber schrumpft der Ort, wo du stehst:*
*Wohin jetzt, Schattenentblößter, wohin?*
*Steige. Taste empor.*
*Dünner wirst du, unkenntlicher, feiner!*
*Feiner: ein Faden,*
*an dem er herabwill, der Stern:*
*um unten zu schwimmen, unten,*
*wo er sich schimmern sieht: in der Dünung*
*wandernder Worte.*[1]

*SPEAK YOU TOO*

Speak you too,
speak as the last,
say out your say.
Speak—
But don't split off No from Yes.
Give your say this meaning too:
give it the shadow.
Give it shadow enough,
give it as much
as you see spread round you from
midnight to midday and midnight.
Look around:
see how things all come alive—
By death! Alive!
Speaks true who speaks shadow.
But now the place shrinks, where you stand:
Where now, shadow-stripped, where?
Climb. Grope upwards.
Thinner you grow, less knowable, finer!
Finer: a thread
the star wants to descend on:
so as to swim down below, down here
where it sees itself shimmer: in the swell
of wandering words.[2]

When asked about his friendship with Paul Celan, Jacques Derrida re-
called his first encounter with him at the *École Normale Supérieure* in Paris
in 1968. Though they had both worked for years at the academy, prior to
1968 the two colleagues had never met. Derrida tells about an incident
that took place at the director's office. Derrida and Celan were meeting
there with some other faculty: "But, sir, do you not remember that the
language instructor we have here is the greatest living poet in the German language?" a German faculty member asked, as the director appar-
ently only knew Celan as a language instructor.[3] In saying, "But, sir, do
you not remember," Celan's colleague evokes the director's attention by a
rhetoric that both rejects his ignorance and draws attention to that which
has not been remembered. Ultimately, though, the German's assertion
of having the "greatest living poet of the German language" in the room
acknowledges the crucial role of language in constructing Nazi Germany.[4] What is evoked but unsaid is the memory of the anti-Semitic ideology in National Socialist Germany. Recognizing that the language instructor is the greatest living poet in the German language seems to be
associated with the irresistible—possibly unconscious—urge to acknowledge that the language does not belong to him. In a way, this colleague
raises the question as to how it became possible for Paul Celan to become
"the greatest living poet in the German language." Examining Paul Ce-

lan's conflict with German as his mother tongue and his persistence in using this language as a vehicle to write poetry again in the aftermath of the Shoah is integral to understanding his oeuvre and his importance in this lexicon of writers, and, for obvious reasons, it is Derrida's name that carries Celan's story with it.[5]

Paul Celan was born in 1920 in Czernowitz, the capital of Bukovina. At that time it was part of Romania, and earlier it had been in Austria-Hungary. Celan's parents insisted that he remain firm in his Jewish roots. His family legacy was strongly Jewish on both sides, and on one side, also Hasidic. His father held Zionist convictions, while Celan's mother instilled her passion for the German language and culture in her son.

Hitler attacked the Soviet Union on June 22, 1941. With the help of Romanian troops, the Nazis retook Bukovina and Czernowitz, which the Soviet Union had held since the invasion of Poland in 1939. Soon arrests and deportations of the Jewish population began. Although Celan asked his parents to hide with him over the weekend, they refused to leave their home and shortly were deported to the camps. Celan managed to escape that deportation, but spent eighteen months in forced labor camps. In the fall of 1942, he received a letter from his mother informing him that his father had been killed by the SS. A few months later, he learned from an escaped cousin that his mother had also been murdered: shot through the back of the neck. In 1944, Celan returned to Czernowitz, which had been liberated by Soviet troops. He moved to Bucharest at the end of the war, resettled in Vienna in December 1947, moved again to Paris, where he remained until April 20, 1970, when he committed suicide by drowning himself in the Seine.[6]

Celan, a Romanian Jew and a survivor, responds in his poetry to the atrocity of the Holocaust by giving testimony to the brutal murder of his parents, the mass murder of millions of anonymous Jewish victims, and attempt to eradicate his Jewish culture.[7] Changing his birth name from Paul Anschel to Paul Celan marks his fundamental dissociation from German culture, a significant shift in his work. His continued writing in the German language, however, seems to profoundly reiterate his painful memories and the suffering imposed upon the victims of the Holocaust. His poems promote access to a certain kind of knowledge, while holding back any simple accessibility or readability of the horror. Acquainting the reader with human suffering through specific figures, Celan alludes to that which is lost and can never be regained. At the same time, Celan's use of German points to the crucial challenge of using his mother tongue to give testimony. Celan explained his loyalty to German to his biographer Israel Chalfen: "Only in one's mother tongue can one express one's own truth. In a foreign language, the poet lies."[8] Celan's poetic work therefore testifies to German as his mother tongue, and most importantly it attests to his own truth.

Paul Celan gives us his paradoxical relationship with German as his mother tongue and his lifelong struggle to write poetry again in the language of the Nazi murderers as reflected in particular passages of his 1958 Bremen Speech. In so doing he presents us with the procedures of making aesthetic choices in the aftermath of the Shoah. His poem "Sprich auch Du," can be seen as an archetype for writing a testimonial *poetics of survival*. "Sprich auch Du" was published in 1955 in a collection of poems called *Von Schwelle zu Schwelle (From Threshold to Threshold)*, the second volume of Celan's early poetry after the Holocaust.[9] In light of the poet's struggle with German after the Shoah, I propose to read the apostrophic "*Du*" as the figure of the maternal voice. To what extent can the poem be read as an allegory of Celan's poetological reflection about his life in creating a poetics of survival? In continuing writing in the German language for purposes of remembrance, one could say it is the maternal aspect of the poet's Jewishness that unfolds within the German. We know that Celan's mother was responsible for his education in the German language and culture. In writing, Celan provides a vibrant remembrance of the Shoah as a means of preserving especially the life of his mother, as well as the lives of millions of anonymous victims.

Yasemin Yildiz's *Beyond the Mother Tongue* focuses on the tension between multilingualism and monolingualism in the literary works of German-language writers. By foregrounding the phenomenon of multilingualism worldwide in the present and past, she draws attention to a most recent development of monolingualism within the era of globalization. Tracing the emergence of a "monolingual paradigm" in late eighteenth century Europe, Yildiz describes the conceptualization of language, identity, and modernity. In the context of German thinkers such as Johann Gottfried Herder, Wilhelm von Humboldt, and Friedrich Schleiermacher, she discusses their fundamental idea that one could communicate only in one's mother tongue. In this regard, she cites Schleiermacher's declaration on language in terms of its creative power: "every writer can produce original work only in his mother tongue [Muttersprache], and therefore the question cannot even be raised how he would have written his work in another language." What Yildiz proposes in her thesis is a "fundamental reconceptualization" of the historical hegemony. In so doing, she borrows Marianne Hirsch's prefix "post" to introduce the term "post-monolingual condition." In this conception, Yildiz describes "the unfolding of the effects of monolingual and not to its successful overcoming or transcendence" and "highlights the struggle *against* the monolingual paradigm." Before elaborating on the notion of the mother tongue, Yildiz underscores that the Latin term *lingua maternal* referred initially to the vernaculars as opposed to the learned language, Latin.[10]

Given the paradigmatic significance of monolingualism, Yildiz argues that the German tradition has played an important role in establishing the role of the mother tongue. In her work, she focuses on German-

speaking writers who were uncomfortable positioned within the paradigm and had to grapple with it to a certain degree. This group includes
pre- and post-Holocaust German-Jewish figures such as Franz Kafka and
Theodor W. Adorno, as well as contemporary writers. According to Yildiz, the emotionally charged term *"Muttersprache"* (mother tongue) arose
in the late eighteenth century in connection with the new notion of "linguistic socialization," at the same time the monolingual paradigm
emerged. What is at stake is the modern notion of the mother tongue that
constitutes a narrative of origin and identity.[11] Recalling Freud's notion
of "family romances," Yildiz reads the modern notion of the mother
tongue as a linguistic family romance that involves affect, gender, kin-
ship, and grounding in language. Through the lens of a present day
study, Yildiz argues "that it is the affectively charged dimension of the
'mother tongue' that accounts for the persistence of the monolingual paradigm and the homologous logic." According to Yildiz, its homologous
logic suggests the need to *work through* the concept of the mother tongue
and "not simply sidestep its force."[12] Situating the idea to *"work through*
the mother tongue" within writing, she coins the term *"beyond* the mother
tongue," thus suggesting that it does not simply mean to write in a "non-
native language or to write in multiple languages. Rather, it means writing beyond the concept of the mother tongue." Drawing on contemporary feminist scholarship such as the work of Julia Kristeva, Barbara
Johnson, and Rosi Braidotti to address the gendered and unique concept
of the mother tongue, Yildiz discusses the various psychoanalytic concepts that emphasize the difference between the maternal and linguistic
in relation to the mother tongue. Through the eyes of today's understanding of the term "mother tongue," she proposes not to ignore the term, but
to think *with* this tongue.

Analysis reveals that the concept of the mother tongue partially emanates from Yildiz's significant work. In contrast to the monolingual paradigm within the German tradition, she makes it unmistakably clear that
"neither Jewish multilingualism nor Jewish monolingualism ever fit easi-
ly into the monolingual paradigm" and that "German has figured more
prominently as a post-Holocaust language." With the focus on Celan's
monolingual assertion of German as his mother tongue, she notes: "Paul
Celan, for instance, famously dismissed the notion of bilingualism in no
uncertain terms and insisted on the singularity of the 'mother tongue' for
his poetry." In the case of Celan, she notes that his acknowledgment of
German as his mother tongue differs significantly from the monolingual
ideal since it was outside ethnic, religious, or national categories. Growing up in a multilingual environment in Czernowitz and speaking several
languages, it was Celan's conviction that German was the only language
in which he could write poetry. In an essay called "Mother Tongue, Holy
Tongue: On Translating and Not Translating Paul Celan," John Felstiner
draws attention to Celan's conviction of monolingualism in writing poe-

try in spite of speaking many languages and translating from French, English, and Russian into German. He cites Celan as saying, "'I do not believe in bilingualness in poetry,' he said, in reply to a question about his linguistic choices. 'Poetry, that is the fateful uniqueness of language'"[13] Despite Celan's attachment to his mother tongue, his concern for using German was deeply rooted in the painful memories that it was also the language of the murderers.

## CELAN'S AFFECTION FOR GERMAN AS HIS MOTHER TONGUE

Celan's affection for German as his mother tongue is best described by Pierre Joris. In his book *Paul Celan: Selections* Joris ascribes the mutual influence of love and strife on the Celanian dynamic. He writes:

> The Celanian dynamic is, however, not simple-minded or one-directional: it involves a complex double movement—to use the terms of Empedocles—of *philotes* (love) for his mother ('s tongue) and *neikos* (strife) against her murderers who are the originators and carriers of the same tongue. He is caught in this love/strife dynamic, the common baseline or ground of which (as *Grund*, ground, but also simultaneously as *Abgrund*, abyss) is the German language, irrevocably binding together both the murdered and the murderer, a dynamic that structures all of Celan's thinking and writing.[14]

Celan problematizes the idea of mother tongue through his use of his own mother tongue. On January 20, 1958, Celan accepted the Literature Prize awarded by the city of Bremen.[15] His speech reveals his experience with and feelings about the German language. Reflecting on Germany's Nazi past, Celan brings up a controversial and a particularly painful subject. He begins his speech with a linguistic analysis of the meaning of "to thank" in the German language:

> *Denken und Danken sind in unserer Sprache Worte ein und desselben Ursprungs. Wer ihrem Sinn folgt, begibt sich in den Beutungsbereich von: "gedenken," "eingedenk sein," "Andenken," "Andacht." Erlauben Sie mir, Ihnen von hier aus zu danken.*[16]

> The words *"denken"* and *"danken,"* to think and to thank, have the same root in our language. If we follow it to *"gedenken," "eingedenk sein," "Andenken,"* and *"Andacht"* we enter the semantic fields of memory and devotion. Allow me to thank you from there.[17]

While acknowledging being the recipient of this prestigious literary award, his remarks allude to the relationship between history and language. Underscoring the common etymological root of the verbs *"denken"* and *"danken,"* Celan draws attention to the inescapable dimension of remembering. This is to say that his phrase, if read in a different way, propels an inviting address: *Erlauben Sie mir, Sie aufzurufen, sich zu erin-*

*nern* (Allow me to call upon you to remember). In other words, the poet's performative gesture, occasioned by the award, situates the significance of remembering the Nazi genocide within language.

In remembering Nazi Germany, Celan brings up a controversial subject to his listeners. Not surprisingly, in his assessment about the German language, the survivor-poet seems to challenge his listeners by using the first-person plural possessive pronoun, *"in unserer Sprache,"* claiming that the German language belongs to both of them. How does one understand Celan's statement in which he declares ownership of German in front of his possibly non-Jewish audience? On the one hand, I would argue, Celan suggests that he has something in common with his listeners. On the other hand, he establishes a distance between himself, a Jewish German-writing poet and his German audience. This distance occurs *in* the German language by depending on that language to attest to an unbearable loss within language. Celan's affirmation of *"unsere Sprache"* stages a paradox. "I have something in common with you," he says to the German audience, and that is the German language. Celan thus verbally affirms the possibility of sharing something. But he also denies this possibility of sharing by remembering the crucial past that they do not hold in common—that splits the audience and the Jewish poet apart—*in* language. What cannot be shared? Celan uses the German language to remind his audience not only of the loss of the dead, but also of the heavy burden that the language of the Nazis, the language of oppression has imposed upon the German language from the years of the Hitler dictatorship.

In the wake of the Jewish history, Celan indirectly addresses fundamental questions pertaining to the racial ideologies and to the destruction of the Jewish German-speaking communities, especially German as the Nationalistic institutionalized mother tongue. In *Linguistics and the Third Reich*, Christopher M. Hutton notes:

> One key aspect of the ideology of the mother tongue was its importance—in the context of Nazism—as an anti-Semitic ideology. For Jews were held to lack a sense of loyalty to their mother-tongue, and were therefore regarded as having an "unnatural" relationship to language. Jews lived in many countries and spoke many tongues; they were rootless nomads with loyalty only to their race. The separation of mother-tongue and race meant that language for them was an instrument of communication only, and a means of entry into other cultures and countries. Furthermore, Judaism was built on veneration of a sacred language, and that sacred language was not the mother tongue.[18]

As we see, Hutton points to the distinct nationalistic construct of the mother tongue and the separateness between Germans and Jews in the Nazis' identity politics. Likewise, in his book *Poetry as Experience*, Philipp Lacoue-Labarthe provides a methodological principle reflected in German politics. Emphasizing the notion of "thinking of history," he claims that the idea itself is essentially German, one that brought about a dimension of nationalism which had never been attained before. According to him, it is remarkable how Germany strove for the possibility of identity for an entire nation.[19] In these historical facts, we can see how the German identity was linked to the centrality of the mother tongue. As a survivor of the Holocaust and as a German-speaking poet, Celan alludes to the sovereign power of the Nazi policies and the ideological differences within language by using the expression *"in unserer Sprache."*

Without explicitly stating it, Celan prompts his audience to remember something for which language has no words.[20] By using the expression *"unsere Sprache,"* Celan acknowledges a relation with another in the absence of that other. In so doing, he binds himself to another—our language—within language as if he were the other. The actual other is absent in the moment of his speech, yet this other is present *in* language through the act of speaking. Celan's conscious and specific use of the plural pronoun *"unsere"* ("our") in relation to the German language thus points to the significance of language as a tool to mark a painful, personal, and collective experience that is linked to German-Jewish history. When he uses the expression *"unsere Sprache,"* he stakes out a narrative space for a world expunged.

In *Sovereignties in Question: The Poetics of Paul Celan*, Évelyn Grossman interviews the Jewish French philosopher Jacques Derrida on questions of Celan's poetic. In the chapter "Language is Never Owned," he reflects on Paul Celan's struggle with the German language emphasizing that his experience, history, and his own experience with the French language cannot be compared with that of Celan. Suggesting that one never appropriates a language, Derrida speaks of Celan's relation to German and his effort "to carry on a hand-to-hand, bodily struggle with it." In discussing that one's signature appears in the linguistic idiom, Derrida claims not only that one's idiom is always "other" but also separates one's linguistic difference from nationalism. For Derrida, Celan produced his own idiom that resists the nationalistic ideology. Referring to Celan's language, Derrida notes that "it seems to me he touches [*touché*] the German language both by respecting the idiomatic spirit of that language and in a sense that he displaces, in the sense that he leaves upon it a sort of scar, a mark, a wound." [21]

Similarly to the history of Celan's narrative, Jacques Derrida describes his relationship to the French language in his autobiographical account *Monolingualism of the Other: or, the Prosthesis of Origin*: "Yes, I only have one language; yet it is not mine."[22] Derrida speaks of his own experience with the French language as his own, his French citizenship, and France's confiscation of this citizenship during the Vichy regime because he was an Algerian Jew. He relates that the "other" monolingualism lacks the attributes ascribed to the mother tongue. Derrida opens up a politics based on the "universal" language theory claiming that language is never owned: "Even when one has only a single mother tongue, when one is rooted in the place of one's birth and in one's language, even than language is not owned." It is of the essence of language that language does not let itself be appropriated. Language does not let itself be possessed but provokes all kinds of movements of appropriation. Derrida writes a sentence with an intrinsic contradiction. On the one hand, he declares to have one language; and on the other hand, he denies ownership of the French language.

Similar to Derrida, the Nazis denied the German-speaking Jews a "natural" relation to German and claimed that they lacked a sense of loyalty to their mother tongue. Comparing the statements of Derrida and Celan, one could say that Derrida's denial of ownership contradicts Celan's claim of ownership. The German-speaking Jewish poet and the French-speaking Jewish philosopher both address the violence done to language and to the people who inhabit it.

Contrary to Derrida's concern with the French language as his mother tongue, Celan's concern affirms his identity as a monolingual writer because a poet can only write in one's mother tongue. Claiming that Celan was neither by nationality nor by mother tongue German, Celan's scholarship confirms the poet's choice to identify German as his mother tongue.[23] Considering the important role of language in each individual life and in the work of these Jewish writers, the question must be raised: How do we understand Celan's direct address claiming ownership of the German language in relation to Derrida's claim that language is not owned?

Following Derrida's theory on language, I suggest that Celan displays his idiomatic signature to deliberately disrupt the predominant fascist thought of ownership in the language of postwar Germany. By using the first-person plural possessive pronoun *"unsere,"* ("our") Celan compels the audience to remember Germany's recent past, in which the language of the Third Reich legally denied Jewish people ownership of the German language in relation to Hitler's race ideology. By saying: *"in unserer Sprache,"* ("in our language"), Celan testifies in front of a German audience to the impossibility of claiming ownership over the German language.

Furthermore, Celan confronts his German audience by establishing in language a reality that pertains to a world of assimilated Judaism in which the German language was part of the cultural tradition. In so doing, he stakes out a narrative space for a Jewish world that no longer exists:

> *Die Landschaft, aus der ich—auf welchen Umwegen! aber gibt es das denn: Umwege?—die Landschaft, aus der ich zu Ihnen komme, dürfte den meisten von Ihnen unbekannt sein. Es ist die Landschaft, in der ein nicht*

*unbeträchtlicher Teil jener chassidischen Geschichten zu Hause war, die Mar-*
*tin Buber uns allen auf Deutsch wiedererzählt hat. Es war eine Gegend, in der*
*Menschen und Bücher lebten.*[24]

The region from which I come to you—with what detours! but then, is
there such a thing as a detour?—will be unfamiliar to most of you. It is
the home of many of the Hassidic stories which Martin Buber has re-
told in German. . . . It was a landscape where both people and books
lived.[25]

By remembering his personal history and that of Eastern European Jews,
Celan describes a landscape where life was happening within the dynam-
ics between Jewishness and the German language. Celan's dilemma describes the devastating history of the Jewish people, and it is especially
his painful memories in relation to the German language that mark his
acceptance speech.[26] What is striking about Celan's address is that on the
one hand he problematizes the role of the German language and on the
other hand he endows language with its undeniable presence: *"Erreich-*
*bar, nah und unverloren blieb inmitten der Verluste dies eine: die Sprache. Sie,*
*die Sprache, blieb unverloren, ja, trotz allem"* ("Only one thing remained
reachable, close and secure amid all losses: language. Yes, language. In
spite of everything, it remained secure against loss").[27]

Celan's words seem to accentuate the role and significance of language in relation to its durable position. Yet he acknowledges language's
complicity in the history of Nazi Germany: *"Hindurchgehen durch die tau-*
*send Finsternisse todbringender Rede"* ("Go through the thousand dark-
nesses of murderous speech").[28] While speaking about the violence of
eliminating innocent Jewish people, Celan points to the linguistics of
National Socialism used in its full capacity to demarcate political power.
In an important essay called "The Realities at Stake in a Poem," Christopher Fynsk discusses Celan's encounter with language after the Holocaust and emphasizes that Celan uses the term *"hindurchgehen"* ("going
through") to describe the survival of language. Its presence thus comes to
be marked by a mode of temporality.[29] Facing the depth of his anguish in
using the language of his mother's murderer, Celan admits his experience of alienation toward the German tongue:

*In dieser Sprache habe ich, in jenen Jahren und in den Jahren nachher, Gedich-*
*te zu schreiben versucht: um zu sprechen, um mich zu orientieren, um zu*
*erkunden, wo ich mich befand und wohin es mit mir wollte, um mir Wirklich-*
*keit zu entwerfen.*

In this language I tried, during those years and the years after, to write
poems: in order to speak, to orient myself, to find out where I was,
where I was going, to chart my reality.[30]

Despite his distance from German, *"in dieser Sprache"* ("in this language"), Celan admits his choice of using "this" language to constitute a

reality in the aftermath of the Nazi atrocities. His reliance on German to write poetry expresses not only the gap between a language *before* and *after* the Shoah, but also gives language a unique role: *"Es war, Sie sehen es, Ereignis, Bewegung, Unterwegssein, es war der Versuch, Richtung zu gewinnen"* ("It meant movement, you see, something happening, being *en route*, an attempt to find a direction").

Celan's complex relation to his mother tongue can best be understood in the following passage. Falsely accused of plagiarism in the so-called "Goll-Affair" in postwar Germany, and devastated by the betrayal of the literary scene in Germany and by postwar anti-Semitism, he nevertheless elucidates his attachment to the German language. Celan wrote a letter to his friend Siegfried Lenz on January 30, 1962:

> And behind all this is more than what one ordinarily describes as a literary intrigue; it's all borne by the evolution of things in Germany (and not only there). My Jewishness probably plays the decisive role in this. You see, dear Siegfried Lenz, I *am* a Jew. By which I also would like to say that I certainly do not regard myself as a representative of Jewishness or as its advocate. I simply *am* it. But I *lived* this Jewishness. And with this living—to which *writing also belongs*—I went where I, following my language, always was and will always be at home: to Germany. . . . I am a Jew. And that I was obliged to experience what . . . I was obliged to experience—ultimately all of these infamies and conspiracies are merely circumlocutions of the cute little word *artfremd* [alien to the race], I am so all the more.[31]

Celan calls attention to the fact that he belongs to the Jewish people and that his identity is Jewish: *"Ich bin Jude"* ("I am Jewish"). He mentions his failure to participate in the Jewish community, yet he asserts his identity and life as a Jew. And he maintains his affection and attachment for the German language: *"dorthin gegangen, wo ich, meiner Sprache nach, immer war und immer zuhause bleibe: nach Deutschland."*[32] No doubt, Celan's statement shows that there is no alternative for him other than using his mother tongue—German. In recalling the historical naming of him as an *"artfremd"* (a Jew), Celan promises to his friend that the commitment to his Jewish identity and conduct as a Jew will be stronger because of Nazism. The survivor-poet stands his ground as a German-speaking Jew. He will not let his language be taken from him, despite all his other losses. Under these specific conditions, Celan's poetic work can be defined by his Jewishness and through his mother tongue. In *Paul Celan, Verweigerte Poetisierung der Welt*, Klaus Voswinckel writes: "Celan uses the language that was handed down to him because there is no other language than the one determined by tradition and burdened by tradition, and because otherwise absolutely nothing can be spoken."[33]

For Celan, writing poetry defines a critical link between language and memory. In the context of his announcement that "language is not lost."

"Sprich auch Du" ("Speak you too") illustrates the survivor-poet's struggle to construct a poem. The poem itself was published in 1950 in *"Von
Schwelle zu Schwelle."* In "Speak you too," the poet tells himself to speak
and to speak as the last.[34] Considering Celan's paradoxical relationship
with German in the aftermath of the Shoah, I suggest that the painful
lyric statement, *"Und duldest du Mutter, wie einst, ach daheim, den leisen, den
deutschen Reim"*[35] ("And can you bear, Mother, as once upon a time, the
gentle, the German, the pain-laden rhyme?"), (*"In der Nähe der Gräber,"*
[Nearness of Graves]),[36] resonates with the theme of the mother characterized in the poem. Celan is, as it were, asking his dead mother for
permission to return to a place of origin for writing poetry. The poet
addresses the split between the past and the present using the word
*"daheim"* ("at home"): on the one hand, Celan suffers the loss of his
"home," that is, the Jewish community in the landscape of Bukovina; and
on the other hand, he suffers the loss of his "home" in terms of the
German language. In "Sprich auch Du," I suggest, Celan takes the poet's
relation to language a step further. Because of the German language's
complicity in the Nazi atrocities, the poem itself can be seen as an aesthetic orientation for writing a testimonial *poetics of survival.* Furthermore,
Celan ties the poet's silence to the spectral presence of his mother inscribed in his poetic voice.

The opening lines center around the subject's gesture calling upon a
"you" to speak. What follows is the request for a specific poem.[37] The
first strophe puts forward a distinct demand linked to the idea of saying a
*"Spruch"* (a saying). Someone addresses a "you," insisting that the addressee must also speak, yet as the last one.[38] Thus, the evocative call
acknowledges that the addressee is able to speak but has not spoken yet.
For the addressor, the silence of the "you" gives rise to an urgency to
perform. The direct address raises a question about the relationship between the addressor and the addressee. One wonders why the addressee
cannot take on the task of speaking. In reading the poem, it also becomes
obvious that the subject "I" never appears in the entire poem. In *Sovereignties in Question,* Derrida reflects on the self-referential self-presenta-
tion that is simply implied by discourses that are not conjugated in the
first-person present tense. He notes: "As soon as I say 'you,' 'your' and so
on, I say or imply 'I.'"[39] Applying Derrida's insight to Celan's poem, the
addresser can be defined as the first-person subject "I." In respect to the I/
you relationship, the question can be posed: How do we understand the
significant role of the addressee in relation to the addressor?[40] As my
reading will soon demonstrate, the addresser can be seen in relation to
German as his mother tongue.

In an essay titled "Apostrophe, Animation and Abortion," Barbara
Johnson discusses the figure of apostrophe and argues that the rhetorical
device gives voice to the absent, dead, or inanimate being in a fictional-
ized way.[41] For her, "Apostrophe is a form of ventriloquism through

which the speaker throws voice, life and human form to the addressee, turning its silence into mute responsiveness."[42] According to Johnson's argument, the imperative call to a "you" "must be read as ventriloquizing of the other."[43] If the addressor's address signifies a demand for the other's creative voice, how do we understand the absence of the addressee? In *Disciplining the Holocaust*, Karyn Ball discusses Kelly Oliver's work on questions of memories, identity, and subjectivity. She foregrounds Oliver's conception of subjectivity: "To conceive oneself as a subject, is to have the ability to address oneself to another, real or imaginary, actual or potential."[44] What is of utmost importance for any reading of the figure of apostrophe is Oliver's observation on self-awareness arguing that self-reflection cannot mean a self-contained, unified self. Instead, she claims "self-reflection must be the reflection of otherness that constitutes the self as subject."[45] Drawing on Oliver's claim, Celan as a survivor, therefore, has been silenced and is searching for a poetic voice. Part of this lacking is owing to Celan's conflict over German as the mother tongue and also as the language of Nazi oppression. But the poetic voice emerges as the conflict is resolved through addressing the mother herself. Therefore, the subject of Celan's poem establishes an imaginary dialogue with his dead mother to constitute himself as a poetic voice. This specific rhetorical act depends upon the poet's ambivalence about using the German language and his inability to speak it in the aftermath of the Shoah. In following Oliver's argument on subjectivity, the poet holds within himself a profound identification with the maternal voice inscribed upon the poetic self. To conceive himself as a subject, the lyric self emerges as Otherness, embedded within the double bind of the mother's tongue and the mother tongue. The calling correlates here with the lack of the poetic voice. The poet is calling upon the spectral presence of his mother to create his poetic voice. What is at stake here is the question of writing itself, particularly after language's complicity in *"totbringenden Reden."* Calling upon the dead mother, that is, her maternal voice, signifies the poet's crisis in speaking. As Ball pointed out, Oliver insists that "the performative aspect of signification" will yield new forms of relationship, with one's self and with others. If the poet aspires to write poetry remembering his mother and all those who died innocently, Celan's poem addresses the poet's search for a new form of relationship with himself emerging as a testimonial "poetics of survival." This means the poet's anticipated longing for his poetic voice resonates in the direct address to an imaginary other. Therefore, the memory of his dead mother is embedded within the metonymic "you."

The roles of language and memory are paramount for Celan's poetic testimony. Calling upon the absent mother signifies a symptom of the subject's crisis in relation to language. Having survived the Holocaust and suffered the death of his parents, in particular the brutal death of his mother, it seems as if Celan seeks to create a poetic space of survival in which both his mother's tongue and mother tongue remain alive. His poetics testify to the capacity of language to transform itself as a language of survival that is bound up with the life of victims who did not survive the extermination camps.[46] In this context, Johnson's article, "Apostrophe, Animation and Abortion," addresses the animating force of direct address through the psychoanalytic work of Jacques Lacan. From Lacan's theory on the verbal development of the infant—"the child's address to his mother not as a person but somehow as a personification of presence or absence, of Otherness itself"—Johnson's response becomes important in the relationship between mother and child. "If apostrophe is structured like a demand, and if demand articulates the primal relation to the mother as a relation to the Other, then, lyric poetry itself, summed up in the figure of apostrophe comes to look like the fantastically intricate history of endless elaborations and displacements of the single cry, "Mama!"[47]

Following Johnson's analysis, the direct address in the poem "Sprich auch Du," ("Speak you too") exemplifies the mother-child paradigm as a model for a Jewish poetics of survival. The poet's address can be read as a "single cry" for his Jewish mother. In the absence of his living mother, the imperative call for the Other symbolically signifies the child's pre-Oedipal phase in which the infant wants to reunite with the mother prior to the formation of the subject's entry into language. Therefore, the memory of his mother's love and her teaching him the German language are embodied within the figure of the "you." In creating a poetic space, the intrinsic identification with the maternal voice unfolds as poetic voice defined by a female aspect. Originating from the spark of the maternal voice, the question can be raised: What happens when the poet is speaking in the mother's presence? Quite simply, the maternal presence prevails over the nationalistic paternal mother tongue used to persecute the Jewish people and other victims communicated in *"totbringenden Reden"* and emerges in the poet's voice. Returning to the mother tongue by remembering his mother's tongue holds the possibility—in effect giving the poet permission—of speaking again in the language of his primordial roots that lie outside the language of oppression.

The commitment to remember the destruction of European Jewry is bound to the making of a poem. For Celan, writing poetry emerges as an encounter between memory and experience. This is to say that the demand of poetry must unfold within specific rules of formation: *"Sag deinen Spruch"* ("Say your saying"). "Sprich auch Du" can be read as the subject's appeal to the maternal voice embedded within the poetic voice. If the poetic voice speaks again, then the demand of poetry for a testimonial poetics of survival is rooted in the memory of the poet's mother, who was brutally shot to death in a Nazi camp.

ARTLESS ART AS TESTIMONY

The notion of *"Spruch"* reintroduces a specific form for the act of speaking. Celan specifically discusses the relation between poetry and art in *"Der Meridian"* in reference to Georg Büchner's *Dantons Tod*.[48] For Celan, poetry is the refusal of art or what is understood as poetics: *"Man komme uns hier nicht mit 'poiein' und dergleichen"* ("Don't come here with *'poiein'* and the like").[49] The survivor-poet questions the work of art by separating it from a philosophical understanding of art claiming that "artless art" means poetry without art.[50] If poems will be made in the distant future, then they will appear as a poetics of survival. At stake is the demand to the reappearing poetic voice to speak as the last (*"Sprich als letzter"*), meaning as the last voice. Felstiner notes that Celan had called himself "one of the last who must live out to the end the destiny of the Jewish spirit in Europe."[51] If language is not lost, then it will speak in relation to its past and its future. Language appearing within the poetic voice will speak as the last voice because it will announce poetry as artless art by binding it to the act of testimony in relation to the Shoah. Language mediated through the poetic voice will at the last, in the end to survive, and it is this testimony of the last one — demanding an impossible response — that emerges as the demand for a new form of poetry.[52]

*Sprich* - (Speak -). Language is called to speak. It is remarkable that the address is clearly concerned with a speaking of the "you" as a reemerged poetic voice in the urgent necessity of speaking. Marco Pajević notes that especially for Celan, the notion of *"Sprechen"* is a means to undo the traditional conflict between the written and the verbal:

> *Dieses Sprechen hebt den Gegensatz auf, der zwischen dem Gesprochenen und Geschriebenen aufgebaut wurde. Denn das Sprechen ist nicht das Lautliche. Das Sprechen besteht in einer Oralität, die im Geschriebenen wie im Gesprochenen anwesend sein kann, die in der Schrift sogar bessere Möglichkeiten hat als ohne sie.*[53]

> This speaking dissolves the opposition that was established between the spoken word and the written word because speech is not merely audible vocalization. Speech consists of an orality that can be present in the written word as well as in the spoken word. And this orality, in fact, has better possibilities in writing than without it.

Pajević situates *"sprechen"* in the context of writing. At the heart of the imperative address lies the return of the poetic voice instructed to compose a poem.

The possible reemergence of the poetic voice bound to "also" speak stands in relation to a very particular task. It is through the particle *"auch"* that we understand the importance of something to speaking. From the poet's perspective, the poems are also prompted to speak, but in contrast to historical speaking. What is perhaps the most remarkable is that the content of a poem can no longer be present as a language about any subject. Language itself is linked to a haunting command in which the making of a saying takes the traumatic event as its object. Language has to return as a language that will speak of the impact of the catastrophic event. At stake is the coming of a saying that must be linked to something meaningful. How do we understand the notion of meaning ("*den Sinn*") in relation to the content of the poem? I would argue that the "you" as language can only give itself as a language that is marked by death. If language can only give in relation to its own damage, a damage that is tied up with the death of other victims, then we have to raise a larger question that stands in relation to language and meaning.

> Speak—
> But don't split off No from Yes.
> Give your say this meaning too:
> give it the shadow.

For language to return depends upon a language that is called to give itself as a new form *after* the event. If language in the form of the poetic voice returns, it will return as a language that stands in relation to its own survival. Language must give itself to the making of a saying. In commenting on the reemergence of language *after* the event, Ulrich Baer observes:

> If Celan does not name a historically specific disaster, this reluctance stems from the shattering realization that every word now exists as a result of it. The desacralization of death and the corruption of language are in fact so strongly linked that signifying this connection with one name or term would wrongly seem to cleanse all other words of their complicity in it.[54]

Baer proposes that the significance of a speaking is linked to the haunting force of the past, and yet language must give itself to the act of testimony. The particularity of speaking is bound up with a specific task of the poet: "*Doch scheide das Nein nicht vom Ja. Gib deinem Spruch auch den Sinn*" ("But don't split off No from Yes. Give your saying this meaning too").[55] Giving voice stands in relation to the effort to appear in the poetic space as a language that excludes neither the "*Nein*" nor the "*Ja*." In relation to the condition of language, "*Nein*" can be seen as a trope of "an unresolved past" and "*Ja*" can be seen as a trope of "speaking again," both of which are inherent in language itself. Language that has outlived the disaster is called upon to give its "*Spruch*." The possessive pronoun *deinem* points not only to the singular appearance of a "you," but also signifies that language can only write what it owns, that is, its intimate relation to the disaster. In this way the opening up of language suggests the possibility of both the "*Ja*" and the "*Nein*" at the same time.

## THE SHADOW OF THE "YOU"

Lacoue-Labarthe evokes a paradigmatic image of the annihilation of the European Jews and others. For him, writing poetry is "writing against the black background," suggesting that "none can escape the era's shadow: a cancer of the subject whether in the ego or in the masses."[56] At stake is the creation of a poetic space that must acknowledge the presence of the shadow: "*Gib ihm den Schatten*" ("Give it the shadow"). There is no doubt that the poetic voice can give the shadow. The presence of shadow bound up with a saying seems to be in reference to an experience. This is emphasized through the colon following "*den Sinn*" ("the meaning"). Strangely, a saying can only take place when language appears as a shadowed one. Language as the poetic voice arises here out of its own shadow. In other words, the creation of the poetic space is inseparable from the experience of time, that is, the time of "*totbringender Rede.*" It also implies that language was complicit in the death of millions of victims. Thus, the presence of shadow holds the inaccessible secret of death within the poetic space.

## TIMELESS TIME

In re-creating a world of atrocity, the poetic space must provide a temporal and spatial dimension in which the shadow can become visible: "*Gib ihm so viel, als du um dich verteilt weißt zwischen Mittnacht und Mittag und Mittnacht*" ("Give it as much as you see spread round you from midnight to midday and midnight").[57] The poetic voice within the poem—and Celan could mean any poem—must expose as much shadow as it knows scattered around within the span of a full day. In *The Discourse of Nature in the Poetry of Paul: The Unnatural World*, Rochelle Tobias points out the importance of time in Celan's poetry: "Time is the element in Celan's poems because the figures they inscribe do not exist in advance of the text but only as a result of it—as a result of the text's exploration of the conditions that make it possible in the first place."[58]

More specifically, the idea of time as a closed circle happens in a clockwise movement of time: "*Mittnacht und Mittag und Mittnacht*" ("midnight and midday and midnight"). The dimension of time as a whole is divided into two halves to articulate the difference between "*Mittag*" ("midday") and "*Mittnacht*" ("midnight") or the difference between day and night. In the movement of time, each particular part of the time dimension seeks the middle of the day as the highest point. Thus, it is the midpoint in which the transition from one time period into another can happen. The notion of time here can be linked to the whole of time in which past and future move through the present time.

Let's return to the command in which the poet's own speech must provide *enough* shadow. Yet, language's shadow in the movement of time is linked to the "giving." In this sense, the re-appearance of language presents itself as shadow. By so doing, the "you" as language experiences its own shadow within itself in the movement of time. It is precisely the non-experience of time within time that marks a timeless experience of the "you" as language. It is important to note that the structure of time repeats itself within the clockwise movement of twenty-four hours. Each hour of time follows another hour of time indefinitely into the future. Thus, the dimension of time can be seen as an infinite movement in which time repeats itself. If the "you" as language experiences the shadow within, and this event happens as a timeless experience in time, then the experience of the "you" can be defined as an experience that repeats itself infinitely. Its shadowed state and its experience of shadow allow language to utter a truth: *"Wahr spricht wer Schatten spricht"* ("Speaks true who speaks shadow"). If someone speaks, the speaking is bound up with the shadow that prevails. Because the act of speaking seems to involve a truth of the past, language must rely entirely on a past that is inseparable from death.

LIFE IN A PLACE OF DEATH

Seeing is pivotal for writing about the landscape of death. The poet's imperative address, inextricably bound up with the maternal voice, stresses the relation between life and death, memory and writing: *"Blicke umher: Sieh, wie's lebendig wird rings. Beim Tode! Lebendig! Wahr spricht, wer Schatten spricht"* ("Look around: see how things all come alive—By death! Alive! Speaks true who speaks shadow").[59] At the heart of the demand lies the request for a specific experience. The act of seeing unfolds as a place in which life and death are inseparable from each other. Looking at death seems to promise life. The sudden appearance of life in the presence of death raises the questions: How can we understand the relation between life and death? How do we understand the interrelation between the figure *"Beim Tode"* and the figure *"Lebendig?"* Given the significance of Derrida's notion of the *revenant* (the French translation of "ghost"), the figure of *"Beim Tode"* ("By Death") points to the history of Nazi Germany and the figure of *"lebendig"* ("alive") denotes the victims' spectral presence. In the *Specters of Marx*, Derrida underscores the appearance of a *revenant* as the presence of the deceased as a ghost. According to him, the crucial presence of the ghost as *revenant* is a spirit that is coming back and can therefore only be defined as an immemorial or eternal past. Derrida's emphasis on the ghost as "this non-present present," this being there of an absent" abides with Celan's tropic expression *"Beim Tode! Lebendig!"* ("By death! Alive!").[60] It is precisely the haunting spectral presence that makes a testimonial "poetics of survival," possible. The creation of a poetic space reflects the coming to life in the face of death.

## MEMORY AND WRITING

The last stanza seems to raise questions about what it means to write in a language that exposes life embedded within death. Celan describes poetry's transposition through figures of travel and change. The literary form for a poetics of survival is described as an inextricable relationship between the apostrophic "*du*" and a "single star."[61]

Poetry's transformation requires a change from one location to another. This is exemplified through the imaginary idea that the place in which the "you" resides is shrinking: "*Nun aber schrumpft der Ort, wo du stehst*" ("But now the place shrinks, where you stand").[62] Driven away by the force of shrinking, the question of "survival" comes up: Where now, shadow-stripped, where? To be called "*Schattenentblößter*" ("Shadow-stripped") means that the poetic voice is deprived of its shadow. It seems as if the act of "shrinking" brings with it the "stripping" of shadow so that the "you" is called ("*Schattenentblößter*"). We can return to the word "*Entblößter*" that emerges from the Latin word "*denudare*," meaning "to expose itself." If the verb "*entblößen*" can be understood in terms of exposing, it means that language exposes itself without shadow as a consequence of the shrinking place. Thus, it is now the specificity of language to expose itself by abandoning its place.

## LANGUAGE APPEARS AS MATERIAL QUALITY

To create a poetic space, the apostrophic "you" is commanded to move in a direction that involves "*steigen*" ("upward") and "*sich emportasten*" ("grope upwards"). Both "*steigen*" and "*tasten*" express an activity that explicitly demands the use of feet and hands. The act of "*steigen*" needs the movement of feet and the act of "*sich emportasten*" needs the movement of hands. The original meaning of the verb "*steigen*" emerges from the two verbs "*schreiten*" and "*gehen*" ("to stride on feet"), which especially stand in relation to the term "*Schritt.*"[63] What is the relation between the act of "*steigen*" and of "*sich emportasten*" assigned to the "you" as language? By imposing a bodily act on language, Celan provides a figurative space that symbolically stands for the rhythmic flow in writing.

Celan figures an analogous process in the development of a poetic space. The instant in which language shifts into a thread is described as a movement of becoming in which the "you" turns into a different form than before: "*Dünner wirst du, unkenntlicher, feiner! Feiner: ein Faden*" ("Thinner you grow, less knowable, finer! Finer: a thread").[64] By turning into *"ein Faden"* language takes the plain form of a material that is defined by its fine texture. It is the material of *"ein Faden"* ("a thread") that can be used for the weaving of a text. Barely visible, the question arises: What is the importance of the "you" appearing as *"ein Faden"* ("a thread") since language presents itself in the form of a line? The notion of a thread becomes significant in terms of its material quality. Language's status in its materiality is clearly seen through the indefinite article *"ein"* that points merely to *a* *"Faden,"* but not to a particular one. It is the essential feature that can be linked to a singular line necessary for creating the textual body of the poem.

## A SINGULAR STAR

The movement of the thread and the star seems to signify the poet's aspiration to construct a poetic space in which the Jewish history of the Nazi atrocity can survive. Celan gives space to a single star that wants to come downward along the thread in order to swim in water:

> *An dem er herabwill, der Stern: Um unten zu schwimmen, unten, Wo er sich schimmern sieht: in der Dünung wandernder Worte.*

> The star wants to descend on: so as to swim down below, down here where it sees itself shimmer: in the swell of wandering words.

The striking figure of the star in relation to the figure of the thread can be seen as a metaphor of survival.[65] In other words, this scene unfolds as the embodiment of a memorial landscape, as, in fact, Celan describes the inextricable relation between Judaism and writing the history of the Holocaust. As a specific historical meaning, we cannot resist alluding to the Jewish badge, "the Star of David," in relation to a haunted Jewish past.[66] Notably, it is the star that explicitly wants to come down along language as a text below where it sees itself gleam: "in the swell of wandering words." What seems to be important is the association of the star with the act of swimming in water. In Latin, *aqua* (water) is linked to time and stands in relation to temporality. If this star, as a reminder of the Shoah, wants to swim deep down below, the figure of swimming suggests a movement in time. It seems as if the possibility for a future writing lay solely in its capacity for commemorating the dead. Jews under Nazism were required to wear a yellow star on their clothing: the star had to be sewn on with thread, not merely pinned on.

It seems as if the construction of a future poetic space is measured by the presence of a single star. Celan allegorizes this in language. Notably, the star sees itself in the water. *"Wo er sich schimmern sieht in der Dünung wandernder Worte"* ("Where it sees itself shimmer: in the swell of wandering words"). How do we understand the figure of *"Dünung wandernder Worte"* ("in the swell of wandering words") in relation to language?[67]

What Celan calls *"Dünung wandernder Worte,"* figures the space of poetry in which language is not settled in any place because it is alienated from any traditional conception of reference.[68] This line suggests that words are deprived of their representational power such as the "nationalistic understanding of mother tongue" and can therefore be opened up to a possibility of giving testimony.[69]

The possibility that language can *give* testimony to the event can be understood in relation to the power of words. If words are defined as words that cannot remain in one place (*"wandernder Worte"*) but move from one place to another, the figure of *"wandern"* can be seen as a language without a stable place or a language without a stable meaning.[70] If the star sees itself in *"der Dünung wandernder Worte,"* then Celan seems to promise the indefinite appearance of words in relation to the Nazi perpetration and annihilation. As we see in the poem, the star never arrives in the water; it only appears as if it did. The possibility for giving a full testimony must always be in the future.

In what follows, I underscore one of Celan's significant theoretical declarations about the status of poetry that coincides with his poetological reflection in "Sprich auch Du." Almost fourteen years after the end of Nazi Germany, the Jewish poet writing poetry in the German language makes a significant statement in the French language. Following the violent student protests in Paris, Celan declares on March 26, 1969: "*La poésie ne s'impose plus, elle s'expose*" ("Poetry no longer imposes, it exposes").[71] I will show how his statement is shaped firstly to renounce hegemonic structures of artistic techniques and secondly to write beyond borders — inside and outside — in the attempt to give testimony.

Notably, Celan addresses the notion of poetry to the exclusion of the poet. Although the poet plays a vital role in the production of the poetry, it seems as if Celan omits any subjective position. Within language, we can see how the eminence of the poet and/or his/her individual existence disappears and how poetry centers its function. At the heart of his announcement lies poetry's altered condition. What we must remember when reading this statement is the root cause of Celan's poetic works after Hitler's Nazi Germany: to testify to the perpetration of genocide against the European Jews. Putting it another way, the result of the historical imposition upon language can be seen in a profound shift distinguished within the previous and current status of poetry. Werner Hamacher notes: "As for 'placing' his [Celan's] work within the body of German imaginative literature after 1945, or against the larger background of international modernism, all we can say is that it occupies a prominent, isolated, and anomalous position."[72] On one hand, Celan gives testimony to a poetry that writes against a poetry imposing itself as a history of ideal objects and national truth. But on the other hand, Celan reveals a different kind of poetry, that is, a poetry of exposition. At stake is not the subjective artistic experience of a poet such as Baudelaire—

*"Mais avec Baudelaire, la poésie françaises s'impose comme la poésie même de la modernité"* —celebrating a historical imposition. Instead, Celan's poetry renounces the poet in order to function in expository ways. If poetry must expose itself in its function, how do we understand its current function? Using Shoshana Felman's terms, Celan seems to proclaim that his poetry exposes itself from *inside* poetry. To understand the notion of "inside," it is necessary to turn toward the two distinctive reflexive verbs *"s'imposer"* and *"s'exposer"* that are significant in relation to Celan's claim.

Although reflexive pronouns are an integral part of the French language, Celan's sensitivity, precision, and command of French can be linked with these two reflexive verbs. I suggest that the grammatical mode of the inextricable relation between the subject and object here inscribes language's falling back toward itself.

In other words, the inseparable relation between language of the past and language in the present is engulfed in this reflexive relation. To differentiate between the present and the past, it seems necessary to ask what actions are involved in both verbs in the subject's agency.

Apart from the fact that they look nearly alike and share the same Latin root, a close examination of the two verbs calls their similarity into question. If we can question their similarity, how do we understand their difference in relation to Celan's poetic declaration? With respect to the mutual Latin root *"pos"* or "to put," the linguistic use is to place or constitute something in the act of the task. The nature of the Latin root *"pos"* suggests the inherent intention to perform a particular task. The use of the reflexive pronoun demands a relation in which subject and object belong together. In a sense, the subject and object cannot escape from each other in seeking a certain action. Perhaps the fundamental difference between the two prefixes *"im"* and *"ex"* can enable us to understand the importance of Celan's poetic declaration.

Examining the reflexive verb *s'imposer* used in the sentence *"La poésie ne s'impose plus"* attests to poetry's past revealing its active intent carried out in the reflexive verb. As a transitive verb, *s'imposer* implies that poetry as an object implicit within the reflexive pronoun *se* directly aims at an indirect object on which it can impose itself. For poetry to force itself upon someone—a potential reader—its historical and subjective imposition can be seen as a rather violent and enclosing act. The significance of the reflexive verb *s'exposer* in *"elle s'expose"* points to a self-contained relation between the subject and object. By the act of presenting itself as object (*"elle s'expose"*), poetry simply situates itself toward a world of possible readers. Within language, it becomes clear that the function of poetry belongs to the inside of poetry and therefore is conditioned by its singularity.

Celan's pronouncement *"La poesie ne s'impose plus, elle s'expose"* in relation to Valéry's statement *"Mais avec Baudelaire, la poésie française s'impose comme la poésie même de la modernité"* can be seen as a statement that defines a poetry *before* and *after* as linked to the Holocaust. Celan leads us back to the past through the negation *"ne . . . plus"* placed around the reflexive verb. What appears here as an adverb of negation (*ne plus*) characterizes the condition of a post-Holocaust poetry. With respect to the reflexivity of the verb, the question now arises whether the relation between subject and object can say something about the status of poetry emerging out of this crucial past. If Celan defines the status of poetry *after* the Holocaust, how can we understand his poetry of exposition?

After the Holocaust, Celan's poetry of exposition can be understood as poetry across borders or, to use Yildiz's term, "beyond" nationality. How do we read Celan's poetry of exposition on the level of language? The poem happens without the poet. It takes place in the mute dimension between language before the Holocaust and language after the Holocaust. Celan's poetry of exposition appears in its muteness, a silence that occurs *inside* language. Philosophers and literary critics such as Theodor Adorno, Maurice Blanchot, Jean-François Lyotard, Ulrich Baer, Werner Hamacher, and George Steiner have engaged with the unintelligibility in the poem, the nature of the poetic voice, and the function of that voice. Geoffrey Hartman's work emphasizes trauma as a function of poetics, exploring the capacity for the "perpetual troping" of that which is unspeakable so as to transmit the experience in language. Since knowledge of trauma remains in the negative, Hartman perceives the need for a mediating representation, especially for a referentiality of the literary kind, which is both less direct and intimately associated with the symbolic or polysemic dimension of experience. Hartman believes that literature's mode of referentiality provides a productive alternative to what Werner Hamacher has framed as a "figure of inversion and/or . . . language is to step in, either as substitute or as prototype, to maintain or to guarantee the possibility of the objective."[73] From the vantage point of exposition, we could say that the silence *inside* poetry exposes itself to an *outside*. It is precisely the force of Celan's figurative language and metonymic uses of language that unfold through the process of reading. Reading derives from poetry's exposition, calling for an intimate relation with a possible reader. In reading, each single figure points both toward and away from the original event. This suggests both the impossibility of grasping the original event and the impossibility of returning to a single meaning. Although each figure, such as the eye or the stone remains in its singular or material form, the process of reading allows us multiple ways to bring the memory of the future.

Paul Celan, as a poet who survived the Holocaust, calls upon the maternal legacy to be able to speak again through his poetic voice. The literary space of the poem expresses the imperative call for the maternal agency within the poet's voice. In order for the poem to function as a testimonial voice, Celan establishes within language and through his mother tongue a vibrant remembrance of the Shoah for preserving the life of his mother and the millions of anonymous victims, and in so doing succeeds in constructing a *poetics of survival.*

## NOTES

1. Paul Celan, "Sprich auch du," in *Gesammelte Werke in Sieben Bänden* (Frankfurt: Suhrkamp Taschenbuch Verlag, 2000), 135. English translation, "Speak You Too," *Selected Poems and Prose of Paul Celan*, trans. John Felstiner (New York and London: W. W. Norton, 2001).

2. Paul Celan, *Selected Poems*, 77.

3. Jacques Derrida, *Sovereignties in Question: The Poetics of Paul Celan*, Perspectives in Continental Philosophy, 44, ed. Thomas Dutoit and Outi Pasanen (New York: Fordham University Press, 2005), 98.

4. Christopher Hutton, *Linguistics and the Third Reich: Mother-tongue Fascism, Race and the Science of Language*, Routledge Studies in the History of Linguistics (New York: Routledge, 1999).

5. See Dorota Glowacka's article "A Date, a Place, a Name: Jacques Derrida's Holocaust Translations," *The New Centennial Review* 7, no. 2 (Fall 2007): 111–39.

6. These biographies of Paul Celan provide a good introduction to the facts of his life: Israel Chalfen, *Paul Celan: A Biography of His Youth*, trans. Maximilian Bleyleben, introd. John Felstiner (New York: Persea Books, 1991); John Felstiner, *Paul Celan: Poet, Survivor, Jew* (New Haven and London: Yale University Press, 1995); Pierre Joris, ed., *Paul Celan: Selections* (Berkeley and Los Angeles: University of California Press, 2005).

7. John Felstiner, *Paul Celan: Poet, Survivor, Jew* (New Haven and London: Yale University Press, 1995).

8. Israel Chalfen, *Eine Biographie seiner Jugend* (Frankfurt: Suhrkamp Verlag, 1983).

9. Jerry Glenn, *Paul Celan* (New York: Twayne Publishers, 1973), 77.

10. Yasemin Yildiz, *Beyond the Mother Tongue: The Postmonolingual Condition* (New York: Fordham University Press, 2012). See also Marianne Hirsch, *The Generation of Postmemory: Writing and Visual Culture after the Holocaust* (New York: Columbia University 2012), 106. Hirsch coined the term "postmemory" in her earlier book *Family Frames: Photography, Narrative, and Postmemory.*

11. As discussed earlier, Philippe Lacoue-Labarthe speaks of Germany as the nation that introduces the importance of identity and nation.

12. Dominick LaCapra introduces the term "working through." See Dominique La Capra, *Writing History, Writing Trauma* (Baltimore: Johns Hopkins University Press, 2001).

13. John Felstiner, "Mother Tongue, Holy Tongue: On Translating and Not Translating Paul Celan," *Comparative Literature* 38, no. 2 (Spring, 1986): 113–36.

14. Pierre Joris, ed., *Paul Celan: Selections* (Berkeley and Los Angeles: University of California Press, 2005), 4–5.

15. Paul Celan, "Ansprache anlässlich der Entgegennahme des Literaturpreises der Freien Hansestadt Bremen, 20 Januar 1958," in *Gesammelte Werke*, 185–86. English translation: Paul Celan, "Speech on the Occasion of Receiving the Literature Prize of the Hanseatic City of Bremen January 20, 1958," in *Collected Prose*, trans. Rosemarie Waldrop: (New York: Routledge, 1986), 34–35.

16. Celan, "Ansprache anlässlich der Entgegennahme," 185–86.

17. Celan, *Selected Poems*, 33.

18. Christopher M. Hutton, *Linguistics and the Third Reich. Mother-tongue Fascism, Race and the Science of Language*, Routledge Studies in the History of Linguistics (London and New York: Routledge, 1999), 5.

19. Philippe Lacoue-Labarthe, *Poetry as Experience*, trans. Andra Tarnowski (Stanford: Stanford University Press, 1999), 7. Originally published in French as *La poésie comme experience* (Paris: C. Bourgois, 1986).

20. Christopher Fynsk, "The Realities at Stake in a Poem," in *Word Traces: Readings of Paul Celan*, ed. Aris Fioretes (Baltimore and London: Johns Hopkins University Press, 1994), 159–84. Fynsk explicitly remarks in his excellent essay that the muteness of language or the impossibility of language to say what has happened can be linked to the collapse of signification.

21. Jacques Derrida: *Monolingualism of the Other; or, The Prosthesis of the Origin*, trans. Patrick Mensa (Stanford: Stanford University Press, 1998), 99–100. (Originally published in French as *Le monolinguisme de l'autre: ou la prothèse d'origine* (Paris: Galilée, 1996).

22. Ibid., 2.

23. Ibid., 100.

24. Celan, *Gesammelte Werke*, 3:185.

25. Celan, *Selected Poems*, 33.

26. Christopher Fynsk, "The Realities at Stake in a Poem," *Word Traces: Readings of Paul Celan*, ed. Aris Fioretes (Baltimore and London: The Johns Hopkins University Press, 1994), 159–84. Christopher Fynsk explicitly remarks in his excellent essay that the muteness of language or the impossibility of language to say what has happened can be linked to the collapse of signification.

27. Celan, *Selected Poems*, 34; Celan, *Gesammelte Werke*, 3:185.

28. Ulrich Baer, *Remnants of Song*: *Trauma and the Experience of Modernity in Charles Baudelaire and Paul Celan* (Stanford: Stanford University Press, 2000), 195–201. I am referring here to Ulrich Baer's exceptional reading, in particular his discussion of Celan's Bremen speech and the role of language "in the absolute *complicity*" in the systematic destruction of the European Jews.

29. Christopher Fynsk, "The Realities at Stake in a Poem," *Word Traces: Readings of Paul Celan*, ed. Aris Fioretes (Baltimore and London: Johns Hopkins University Press, 1994), 162.

30. Celan, *Selected Poems*, 34; Celan, *Gesammelte Werke*, 3:186.

31. Barbara Weidemann, *Paul Celan—Die Goll-Affäre* (Frankfurt am Main: Suhrkamp, 2000).

32. Ibid., 558.

33. See Klaus Voswinckel, *Paul Celan: Verweigerte Poetisierung der Welt Versuch einer Deutung*, (Heidelberg: Lothar Stiehm Verlag, 1974). Original text: "*Bei Celan wird die tradierte Sprache aufgegriffen, weil es eben keine andere gibt als die, die von der Tradition bestimmt und belastet ist, und weil es anders gar nicht ausgesprochen werden kann,*" 56.

34. John Felstiner, *Paul Celan: Poet, Survivor, Jew* (New Haven and London: Yale University Press, 1995), 78. Celan's translator Paul Felstiner suggests that the poem "Sprich auch Du," is a response to a review in April 1954 of his *Mohn and* Gedächtnis (1952) in the respected *Merkur*.

35. Ibid., 24.

36. Celan, *Gesammelte Werke*, III, 20.

37. Lyotard discusses the impossibility of address in the aftermath of the Shoah. It is the absence of an addressee that makes it impossible to institute a common world. See Jean-François Lyotard, *The Differend: Phrases in Dispute*, trans. Georges Van Den Abbeele (Minneapolis: University of Minnesota Press, 1988).

38. In German, the personal pronoun *du* (you) is used to signify a certain intimacy with another person. To engage with another in the form of a personal pronoun *du* affirms that both the addressor and addressee possibly stand in a very close relation with each other. Using the personal pronoun *du* also signifies the presence of a singular person. Thus, the addresser who addresses this particular but unidentified "you" in his or her singularity can be defined as someone who must be intimate with the addressee.

39. Derrida, *Sovereignties in Question*, 89.

40. Émile Benveniste closely ties the question of subjectivity to the use of pronouns, signifying that no sense of subjectivity is possible without language. For him, the pronoun "I" constitutes itself as a subject by entering into a relationship with another

pronoun. The "I" is impossible without the "you." This dialogic relation that constitutes the subject on the basis of the interrelation between "I" and "you" is significant
in the context of the poet's relation to language. According to Benveniste, the reciprocity of this pronoun relationship shows the linguistic basis of subjectivity within
speech.

41. Barbara Johnson, "Apostrophe, Animation and Abortion." *Diacritics* 16, no. 1,
(Spring 1986), 28–47.

42. Ibid., 30.

43. Petra Schweitzer, "Death in Language," in *After Representation? The Holocaust,
Literature, and Culture,* ed. R. Clifton Spargo and Robert M. Ehrenreich, (New Brunswick and London: Rutgers University Press in association with the United States Holocaust Memorial Museum, 2010), 59–74.

44. Karin Ball, *Disciplining the Holocaust* (Albany: State University of New York
Press, 2008), 171. See also Kelly Oliver, *Witnessing beyond Recognition* (Minneapolis:
University of Minnesota Press, 2001), 219.

45. Ibid.

46. Cathy Caruth, "Parting Words: Trauma, Silence and Survival" in eds. Michael
Rossington and Anne Whitehead, *Between the Psyche and the Polis: Refiguring History in
Literature and Theory* (Farnham, UK: Ashgate, 2000), 77–96. Caruth discusses the prob-
lems of language in trauma and the departure of a new language related to the future.

47. Barbara Johnson, *Mother Tongues: Sexuality, Trials, Motherhood, Translation* (Cambridge, MA: Harvard University Press, 2003), 38.

48. Celan indicates this expression in his acceptance speech of the Georg Büchner
Prize. He specifically discusses questions of art referring to Büchner's *Dantons Tod.* He
discusses poetry in relation to a self-encounter. According to Celan, poetry emerges
from a place where it is liberated from art. He makes clear that the poetic self comes
forth only in the movement toward the other.

49. Celan, *Selected Poems,* 26; Celan, *Gesammelte Werke,* 3:177.

50. Michael G. Levine, *A Weak Messianic Power: Figures of a Time to Come in Benjamin,
Derrida, and Celan* (New York: Fordham University Press, 2014), 37–62. See especially
Levine's remarkable chapter "Pendant: Celan, Büchner, and the Terrible Voice of the
Meridian." He discusses in detail Celan's 1960 Meridian address. In the section, "Poetic Interventions," Levine discusses Celan's understanding of the textual event, claiming that the notion of *Wiedergeburt,* "a movement of circular repetition," is associated
at the very beginning of the Meridian with the movement of "art."

51. Felstiner, 80.

52. Klaus Voswinckel, *Paul Celan: Verweigerte Poetisierung der Welt Versuch einer Deutung* (Heidelberg: Lothar Stiehm Verlag, 1974). Voswinckel speaks of the end of art in
comparing Novalis to Celan. The end of art coincides with the refusal of the most
romantic form of poetry.

53. Marco Pajević, *Zur Poetik Paul Celans: Gedicht und Mensch—die Arbeit am Sinn*
(Heidelberg: Universitätsverlag Winter, 2000), 129–30. Pajević writes, "Celan's poems
talk about the 'written speech' of a poem. The written word is preserved in the inscription." The English translation is by Howard Fine.

54. Ulrich Baer, *Remnants of Song: Trauma and the Experience of Modernity in Charles
Baudelaire and Paul Celan* (Stanford: Stanford University Press, 1996), 179.

55. Celan, *Selected Poems,* 77; Celan, *Gesammelte Werke,* 1:135.

56. Lacoue-Labarthe, 8.

57. Baer, *Remnants of Song,* 189. Celan, *Selected Poems,* 77; Celan, *Gesammelte Werke,*
1:135. Baer discusses time in Celan's poetry: "Celan's poems are marked by their time
and dates, even when this time is not named directly and this date not explicitly given
in the poems. The poem's openness to time, however, depends on its absolute openness, and thus on the possibility that each inscription of such time loses its singularity
at the moment when it opens the poem to remembrance and commemoration."

58. Rochelle Tobias, *The Discourse of Nature in the Poetry of Paul: The Unnatural World*
(Baltimore: Johns Hopkins University Press, 2006), 13.

59. Celan, *Selected Poems*, 77; Celan, *Gesammelte Werke*, 1:135.

60. Jacques Derrida, *Spectres of Marx* (New York: Routledge, 2006). (Originally published in French as *Spectres de Marx*. Paris: Éditions Galilié, 1993).

61. Gerald L. Bruns, *Maurice Blanchot: The Refusal of Philosophy* (Baltimore and London: Johns Hopkins University Press, 1997), 81–101. See especially chapter 4, "Blanchot/Celan: *Unterwegssein*" in which Bruns discusses questions of poetry in Blanchot and Celan in relation to movement.

62. Celan, *Selected Poems*, 77; Celan, *Gesammelte Werke*, 1:135.

63. Celan, *Gesammelte Werke*, 3:189. Celan uses the notion of *Schritt* to explain the way in which poetry frees itself from the previous understanding of art.

64. Celan, *Selected Poems*, 77; Celan, *Gesammelte Werke*, 1:135.

65. Ibid., 289. Baer notes that Celan has "inseminated" the darkness with star-poems after the Holocaust.

66. Raul Hilberg, *The Destruction of the European Jews* (New York and London: Holmes & Meier, 1985).

67. Rochelle Tobias speaks of Celan's "self-reflexive" work.

68. Herman Rapaport, *Is There Truth In Art?* (Ithaca and London: Cornell University Press, 1997), 1–57. Rapaport explores the question of art in relation to the Western tradition. He especially discusses Heidegger's understanding of art that is useful in understanding the ways in which Celan sets himself apart from Heidegger, although his poetry is influenced by him.

69. On the status of words, see Sarah Kofman, *Smothered Words*, trans. Madeleine Dobie (Evanston: Northwestern University Press, 1998).

70. Joseph Roth, *The Wandering Jews: The Classic Portrait of a Vanished People*, trans. Michael Hofman, comment, Elie Wiesel (New York: W. W. Norton, 2001). Originally published as *Juden auf der Wanderschaft* (Amsterdam/Köln: Verlag Allert de Lange and Kiepenheuer & Witsch, 1976/1985). The idea of the "wandering Jew" has been discussed in many literary works, in particular in relation to the rootlessness of the Jew.

71. Ulrich Baer, *Remnants of Song: Trauma and the Experience of Modernity in Baudelaire and Paul Celan* (Stanford: Stanford University Press, 2000). Baer offers a close reading of Celan's "one-sentence revision of Valéry's comment on Baudelaire" in 1924: "*Mais avec Baudelaire, la poésie française. . . . S'impose comme la poésie même de la modernité*" (But with Baudelaire, French poetry imposes itself as the very poetry of modernity). In his encounter with Valéry's comment on Baudelaire as a poet who breaks free of the French tradition, Baer argues that "Baudelaire's work inaugurates the very notion of modernity by defining modernity as something that is not site specific and instead aspires, for the better or the worst, to level all differences that result from the contingencies of time and place." With respect to Baudelaire's poetry imposing itself as "the truth of modernity," Baer notes that Celan responds in the French language in order to mark "the distance between his own German poetry of 'exposition'" and the tradition inaugurated by the earlier French poet. Baer gives us an insight into Celan's claim undoubtedly linked to his vicious past with Germany. Thus, in his close reading of Celan's declaration on poetry, he shows how Celan distances himself through language from the literary and philosophical German tradition. By intentionally using the French language, Celan interrupts Heidegger's concept of poetry first as imposing act that founds history and second as expository act of "setting—into—work of truth (*ins-Werk Setzen der Wahrheit*). According to Baer, Celan's recourse to the French language signifies the gesture of a new poetry breaking with a "National Aestheticism."

72. Celan's break with the German tradition and Heidegger's understanding of it by escaping into the French language suggest yet another reading of the declaration, accentuating its poetic testimony.

73. Paul Celan, *Poems of Paul Celan: A Bilingual German/English Edition,* trans. and introd. Werner Hamburger (New York: Persea Books, 2002), xix.

# THREE

## The Maternal Function of Giving Testimony

### Charlotte Delbo

The literary Holocaust testimonies of Charlotte Delbo (1913–1984) reso-
nate with the perpetration of female prisoners in the concentration camps
and their lives as survivors after liberation. As a non-Jewish survivor of
Auschwitz-Birkenau and Ravensbrück, who was imprisoned as a consequence of her political involvement in the French resistance movement,
her skillful literary writing brings individual and collective experiences
of the concentration camps to people's consciousness. *"Il faut donner à
voir"* underscores Delbo's impetus to go on living after surviving the
Nazi camps and her repetitive avowal to transmit the knowledge she
acquired in *l'univers concentrationionnaire*.[1] Acknowledging that literature
serves as a vehicle to narrate the horrors of victimization, the survivor
writer states: *"Je me sers de la literature comme d'une arme, car la meance
m'apparaît trop grande"*[2] ("I use literature as a weapon, because the threat
appears very great to me").

In order to better understand Delbo's work within a larger context of
literary representations of testimonies, one must appreciate the spirit of
the woman who would one day publish her memoirs. Delbo was born in
Vigneux-sur-Seine, near Paris, in 1913, and developed an affinity for theater and politics in her formative years. By 1932, she had joined the
French Young Woman's Communist League and in 1934 she married
fellow traveler Georges Dudach, who would soon become a member of
the French resistance. As a non-Jewish French citizen Delbo also decided
to join the resistance. Maintaining her interest in the theater while also
being active in progressive politics led her to work as Louis Jouvet's

assistant.[3] Delbo was on tour with his theater company in Latin America in 1940 when the Wehrmacht first invaded France. In 1941, while still on tour in Brazil with Jouvet's troupe, Delbo received the news that friends from the resistance had been arrested in France. Against Jouvet's advice, she returned to Paris to be with her husband and other members of the French Resistance. In March 1942, Delbo and her husband were arrested for producing anti-German fliers. Both of them were handed over to the Gestapo and imprisoned. Dudach was executed at Mont Valérain on May 23. Delbo was arrested and spent the next ten months in French prisons. In 1943, she was sent to Auschwitz-Birkenau in a convoy of 230 women, most of whom were involved in the French Resistance.[4] On January 7, 1944, she was transferred to Ravensbrück and stayed there until her liberation by the Red Cross in 1945. After liberation she went first to Sweden before returning to Paris at the end of June 1945, where she remained until she died of lung cancer in 1985.

Immediately after returning from the camps, Delbo began writing *Aucun de nous ne reviendra* (*None of Us Will Return*), the first volume of her *Auschwitz et après* (*Auschwitz and After*), originally published in French, followed by two more volumes titled *Une connaissance inutile* (*Useless Knowledge*) and *Mesure de nos jours* (*The Measure of Our Days*).[5] In *Le convoi du 24 janvier* (1965), Delbo testified to her imprisonment with 230 women, out of whom, only Delbo and 48 others survived. Critics of Delbo's work have pointed out the survivor's ability to take the reader inside the space of horror and to engage them emotionally in different perspectives on suffering. Among the many critics of Delbo's fictional work are the pioneering analyses of Lawrence L. Langer, Michael Roth, and Brett Ashley Kaplan. These very influential scholars focus on Delbo's creative writing in the context of larger theoretical questions of historical representation, paying particular attention to issues of memory in the context of extreme experiences. In her article "Aesthetic Survival: Paul Celan, Charlotte Delbo, and 'Living next to Auschwitz,'" Kaplan claims that the aesthetic quality of Delbo's writing was greatly influenced by her theatrical training. She writes:

> Delbo chose to speak the words needed to tell the story of her incarceration by creating beautiful literary testimonies that combine drama, prose, and poetry into reflections on her painful past and the struggle to represent those experiences to those of us who did not live through the horror of the camps. She thus offers us both descriptions of the past and the theories of memory that illuminate how that past continues to live next to and in survivors.[6]

As Kaplan keenly describes, Delbo's literary aspiration for taking the reader inside the spaces of suffering makes visible the invisible. In his book *Traumatic Realism: The Demands of Holocaust Representation*, Michael Rothberg challenges the traditional scholarly approach between the realist and antirealist position in terms representing the traumatic event. Arguing against the opposition between factuality or unrepresentability of the Holocaust, Rothberg introduces the term "traumatic realism" as a new mode of representation writing trauma. For him, "traumatic realism [. . .] seeks to bring forth, 'traces of trauma,' to preserve and even expose the abyss between every day reality and real extremity."[7] In his reading of Delbo's work, Rothberg highlights the survivor's writing, that is, "the relationship between the ordinary and the extreme under traumatic circumstances."[8]

In Delbo's trilogy of memoirs, which mark a process of fragmentation, the survivor writes about her and other women's experiences in Auschwitz and Ravensbrück: the shock of arriving at the extermination camps, the daily struggle of men and women in the death camps, and the liberation. In her first volume, *None of Us Will Return* (1965) the survivor raises the question of what it means to return from the concentration camps and, even more profoundly, whether such a return is truly possible. Within a larger framework, individual and collective stories of experiences inside the camps express the difficulty of surviving beyond each individual atrocity—each event that already questions the possibility of leaving behind, or returning from, the camp experience. Delbo re-creates a traumatic scene to draw attention to the sudden and unexpected return of traumatic memories. Karein K. Goertz's essay: "Body, Trauma, and the Rituals of Memory: Charlotte Delbo and Ruth Klüger," concurs that Delbo makes the female body the main protagonist in her memoirs, claiming that "the body becomes the dominant stage upon which traumatic experiences are reenacted."[9]

In his introduction to *Auschwitz and After*, the English translation of Delbo's *Auswitz et Après*, Lawrence Langer describes Delbo's memory theories, attesting to Delbo's acknowledgment about two selves, "her Auschwitz self and her post-Auschwitz self."[10] Langer highlights Delbo's differentiation between *mémoire ordinaire* and *mémoire profonde* that he translates into "common memory" and "profound memory." Delbo underlines the fact that her external memory, that is, the "me" of living now, is inextricably bound up with her deeper memory, the internal "me" of living in Auschwitz. It is within this self-described framework that Delbo's testimonial writing has been most closely examined, for it is in these testimonies that the author's claims of the role of memory in understanding the relationship between her past and present self are made visible.

Delbo's command of figurative language is particularly evident in the story "*La jambe d'Alice*" ("Alice's Leg"). The leg comes to represent the singularity of an event imposed upon female prisoners and a means through which Delbo addresses the impact of trauma on the psyche of victims. The interrelation between external and deep memory is particularly exemplified in the stories of "*Le même jour*" ("The Same Day"), and

"*La jambe d'Alice*" both of which appear early on in the first volume of
Delbo's trilogy, *None of Us Will Return*. What becomes important in "*La
jambe d'Alice*" is the unexpected return of a particular traumatic event
embedded within a wooden leg that seems to be alive. The story centers
on a group of women who encounter a wooden leg and assume that this
anonymous prosthesis is the artificial leg of their dead friend Alice.[11]
How is it possible for a wooden leg to be alive? To understand the impact
of trauma as seen in "Alice's Leg," a brief synopsis of the fragment titled
"*Le même jour*," which precedes the story of "Alice's Leg" provides insights into how Delbo constructs the history of a past event central to
understanding traumatic memory.[12]

In the context of the vast number of studies on the pathologies of
memories, early works by Jean-Martin Charcot and Pierre Janet provided
the groundwork for interpreting Sigmund Freud's theory on trauma,
which formed the basis for much of the work that followed.[13] In *Beyond
the Pleasure Principle* (1920), Freud defines the concept of trauma as a
response to people's suffering after having survived near-death experiences. In his theory, he claims that the unexpected and overwhelming
event is not experienced at the time it happens but only after a delay of
time. Freud describes how in trauma the psyche of the victim is wounded
because the surprising return of the event—in a form or at a moment that
does not necessarily replicate the original circumstances of the trauma—
brings the victim back into the situation of the catastrophe. Cathy Caruth's influential books, including the edited volume, *Trauma: Explorations in Memory* (1995) and the monograph *Unclaimed Experience: Trauma,
Narrative and History* (1996) mark not only her remarkable reading of
Freud's *Beyond the Pleasure Principle*, but also provide a groundwork for
thinking about the surprising, unexpected impact of trauma to rethink
notions of experience, and the role of language in post-traumatic accounts, in particular the role of literature in mediating and remediating
trauma.[14] Delbo's writing is remarkable for its deft interweaving of figurative language with its implicit grasp of what scholars like Caruth have
concluded: that the pathological symptom of post-traumatic stress disorder is not so much a symptom of the unconscious, but rather a symptom
of history. If, as Caruth observes, "the traumatized carry an impossible
history within them, or they become themselves the symptom of a history
they cannot entirely possess," then Delbo's decision to recount one of the
more brutal episodes of her past traumatic experiences by giving life to
the disembodied leg of Alice demonstrates the author's ability to craft a
space within language and within herself where past and present can
perhaps coexist, even if they can never be historically or emotionally
reconciled. Delbo's writing is a critical space and critical means through
which she can resist the tendencies in literature—and in life—to explain
away the inexplicable through more common narrative tropes such as
foreshadowing and back shadowing.[15]

Before the appearance of Alice's leg *behind* Block 25, Alice, a prisoner of the concentration camp, has been stripped of her life *in front* of Block 25. In understanding the difference between the place *in front of* and *behind* Block 25, the reader needs to return to "*Le même jour,*" the story that precedes "*La jambe d'Alice.*"[16] In this narrative, the reader learns of a singular event that happened *in front* of Block 25. The opening scene recounts how female prisoners who were outside the gates had been forced to run back inside the block gates to save their lives. In the face of human abuse, the narrative describes the perpetuating violence against the women who have been out in the cold all day and points to their physical exhaustion:

> *Nous marchions. Des automates marchaient. Des statues de froid marchaient. Des femmes épuisées marchaient. Nous allions, quand Josée, dans le rang qui nous précédait, se tournant vers nous, dit: "Quand vous arriverez à la porte, il faudra courir."*[17]

> We were walking. Walking automatons. Walking ice statues. Exhausted women were walking. We were on our way when Josée, in the preceding rank, turned towards us to say: "When you get to the gate you'll have to run."[18]

Delbo recounts a situation in which the act of running becomes a matter of life and death. One of the victims tells about her experience: "*Je ne sais pas si j'avais compris, qu'il fallait courir parce qu'il y allait de la vie. . . . Nous courions. Nous courions.*"[19] ("I do not know if I had understood that running was a life-and-death matter. . . . We ran. We ran.")[20] In the story, Alice, who has a wooden leg, is unable to run fast and it is precisely this disabled leg that makes her fall. Hélène, who tries to help Alice, also falls. Hélène's role was to draw Alice along, but she was unable to get up anymore. Hélène must come to terms with the impossibility of carrying her back to the camp. She wants to help Alice but knows she cannot save them both, and she is encouraged to leave her friend behind to save her own life. This act weighs on Hélène, and she expresses to others the immediacy of the threat of death for her and Alice: "*Laisse-la. Laisse-la. Je me suis remise à courir. J'ai dû abandonner Alice. Est-ce qu'on ne peut pas aller la chercher?*" ("Leave her alone. Leave her. I started running again. I had to abandon Alice. Can't we go get her?").[21] Alice fell because her wooden leg hampered her movement. Everyone had to keep moving: "*Ne restez pas devant le 25*"[22] ("Don't linger in front of block 25"). The imperative to get away from Block 25 tells the women what to do: they must leave Alice behind, they must move away from her.

Freud's concept of trauma points to a belated return of the traumatic experience and its surprising impact against the victim's will. The temporal delay between the time of the traumatic event and the return to it can be seen in the construction of the narrative. The traumatic event of Alice's cruel dying happened in front of Block 25, *before* her leg reappears behind Block 25 *after* the event, that is, *behind* Block 25. In this way, the appearance of Alice's leg becomes the connection between the catastrophic event of the past and the present moment. Victoria Stewart argues that an individual cannot negotiate between "before" and "after" because the "after" was never to happen.[23] She explains that survivor's testimonies—especially Delbo's poetic prose—subvert the logic of total annihilation of the Nazi system. In her insightful essay on writing after surviving, Stewart makes the point that writing itself demonstrates the resistance to radical silencing. Following the narrative of "The Same Day," Delbo recounts that all the women who were left in front of Block 25 died. Alice's death reveals itself as an individual trauma: *"La plus longue à mourir a été Alice"*[24] ("The one who took the longest time to die was Alice"). Delbo sets Alice's brutal dying apart from all the other victims who were left in the field to die. Dying in front of all the women turns her death into a shared experience for the ones who had to leave her behind. Therefore, the return of Alice's leg emerges not only as a surprise but also as an enigma because it appears *behind* Block 25.

Furthermore, the importance of Alice's leg is not only its emergence but also the place in which it reappears. The narrative gives no explanation of how the leg was moved from one place to another. What does it mean to see Alice's leg unexpectedly *behind* Block 25? Surely, something must have happened in-between. It is significant that the appearance of the leg marks a shift between places—attached to Alice's body *in front of* Block 25 rather than detached *behind* Block 25. What is the relation between these two places that opens up an in-between space where the unspeakable took place? The sudden appearance of Alice's leg *behind* Block 25 can be linked to the dynamic process of trauma and its seemingly timeless dimension unfolding over time. In the context of trauma, Caruth explains that "the pathology of trauma consists, rather, solely in the *structure of experience* or reception: the event is not assimilated or experienced fully at the time, but only belatedly in its repeated *possession* of the one who experiences it. To be traumatized is precisely to be possessed by an image or event."[25] According to Freud, she notes, the force of traumatic events lies in their belatedness.[26] Therefore, an anonymous wooden leg brings back, in an estranged form and with a new and incomprehensible element, the knowledge that the women thought they possessed: that Alice fell in another place with her wooden leg and was abandoned by them. As a reminder of Alice, the leg seems, now, in its strange reappearance and afterlife, a link not to the living Alice but to her absence as it lives on through this detached prosthesis.

Delbo seems to construct the unexpected occurrence of a wooden leg to preserve a disrupted collective memory of female prisoners through the trope of "Alice's Leg." When one of Alice's friends, little Simone, encounters the leg, she returns to all the other women and calls them to come and look: *"La jambe d'Alice est là-bas. Venez voir"* ("Alice's leg is over there. Come see").[27] As we will see later, Delbo's literary language embodies the incomprehensible return of an extreme event within the trope of Alice's leg. Calling all the other women gives voice to the underlying trauma, that is, the shock of seeing a disembodied leg without Alice's suffering body in front of their eyes. The traumatic event of Alice's individual death, as it is represented through the women's encounter with the emergence of a wooden leg is heightened, moreover, by the explicit contrast with a pile of dead bodies that the women see every day and do not notice:

> *Derrière le block 25, il y avait la morgue, une baraque de planches où l'on entassait les cadavres sortis des revirs. Empilés, ils attendaient le camion qui les emporterait au four crématoire. Les rats les dévoraient. Par l'ouverture sans porte, on pouvait voir l'amoncellement de cadavres nus et les yeux luisants des rats qui apparaissaient et disparaissaient. Quand ils étaient trop, on les empilait dehors.*[28]

> Behind block 25 was the morgue, a wooden hut where they piled up the dead hauled from the charnel house. Stacked one on top of the other, the corpses awaited the truck that would carry them to the crematorium. The rats were devouring them. Through the doorless opening one could see the heap of naked corpses and the glittering eyes of the rats darting to and fro. When there were too many of them, they were piled up outside.

The fact that the visibility of Alice's leg is shocking while seeing the dead bodies piled on top of one another raises a question as to its particular significance, a significance that seems to exceed the fact of death and points toward something about Alice's death in particular that remains to be understood. Indeed, Alice's leg comes to figure the way in which a singular event—Alice's isolated and excruciating dying—has precisely been *missed*. In Caruth's words, the *missed event* characterizes trauma as the event that is not assimilated or experienced fully at the time, but only belatedly in its repeated *possession* of the one who experiences it. In this light, the inability to experience the traumatic event testifies to the radical rupture of temporal continuity. In the context of Alice's story, it is the sudden involuntary memory both of her dying and also of her absence that returns with the appearance of the prosthetic leg. The story asks us to confront both the incomprehensibility of this specific kind of death and its larger figurative significance for the nature of annihilation in the Holocaust. The leg stands not only as a reminder for the women who are in the camp, but also as a figure for readers who must come to face—through a unique language of trauma constructed by Delbo—an event that nonetheless can never be fully comprehended.

## A Haunting Wooden Leg

Haunted by the emergence of this particular wooden leg, which is identified as Alice's leg, the women question the separation between the body and the leg: "*Elle a dû se détacher d'Alice morte*" ("It must have detached itself from the dead Alice").[29] These words signify the departure of Alice's leg from her body after she died and its reemergence behind Block 25. In response to the enigmatic appearance of the leg, this particular separation represents a *gap* between what is known and what is unknown. The gap is linked to both the time of the extreme event and to the radical discontinuity of the traumatic experience. It is the impossibility of integrating the experience into normal patterns of memory that characterizes the relation between knowing and not knowing. The women's fascination with the appearance of a wooden leg and the ambivalence of seeing it without Alice generates a self-explanatory response: "It must have detached itself from the dead Alice." This moment of detachment is experienced as enigmatic and unknown. It is the "not knowing" how the leg arrived at the new place that defines the condition of Alice's leg. If Alice's leg detached itself from Alice's body, it arises for the women as a part of Alice, but remains without her. Alice's leg appears *now* as a part that lacks the body to which it was attached. Departed from its original place and detached from Alice's body, it is embodied anew: "*Couchée dans la neige, la jambe d'Alice est vivante et sensible*" ("Lying in the snow, Alice's leg is alive and sentient").[30] Paradoxically, the very life within Alice's leg marks the absence of Alice's dead body. The appearance of Alice's leg thus raises the question: Where is the body? It is the absence of Alice's body that makes the appearance of Alice's leg so important. What, then, is the function of Alice's leg in relation to her death? And what does it mean that Alice's death is marked, and in a sense commemorated, through the apparent and inexplicable "life" of the leg?

## A Wooden Leg—A Prosthesis

What distinguishes Alice's leg from Alice? Alice's leg appears as a part of her but apart from her. In the story entitled "*Le même jour*," Delbo writes of a time when Alice's wooden leg was connected with her body. In medical terms, prosthesis is defined as an artificial extension that replaces a missing body part.[31] Thus, Alice's artificial device substitutes for an amputated leg allowing Alice as the amputee to move with two legs. By this supplementary function, Alice's leg can be defined as both a part of an organic structure—a human body, and an inorganic structure—an artificial prosthesis. Alice's leg was, then, originally an inorganic supplement to a living body. Yet, in the narrative of "The Same Day," it is precisely Alice's artificial limb that contributed to her falling and dying.

Now, separated from her and described as "living," the leg is a different kind of supplement, not to her life but to her death. In describing the leg as living, the living quality of Alice seems to have been transferred to her leg, yet it is not the vibrant life of the human being, but a peculiar afterlife that cannot be said to be properly organic or inorganic. Thus, in Alice's leg there resides a life that is different from a fibrous cellular life. How can we understand the notion of *life* in Alice's leg in relation to Alice's death? It is through Alice's death that her leg becomes alive. Both life and death are embedded within Alice's leg once Alice has died. If Alice's leg is a supplement to life, then it is also a supplement to death. The life of the leg as a visual image might indeed be understood as the haunting *life* of a traumatic experience returning as a belated response and recognition to the women who survived it. By seeing Alice's leg, the unbearable traumatic experience recurs—and haunts those who experienced it.

## A PLACE OF DEATH

Delbo's description of this reality of corpses stacked upon one another and being devoured by rats situates Alice's wooden leg within the site of mass murder. What seems to be shocking is the fact that the ones who are still alive are brutally exposed to a situation in which the human body turns into an inanimate object doomed to disappear by way of the crematorium. The women who survive remain within a landscape of death. How do we understand the figure of the wooden hut? Normally, a wooden hut provides a space for storing material objects, for finding shelter. Here, however, the image is most striking because this wooden hut holds individual dead bodies until they are turned to ashes in the crematorium. It soon becomes evident that the figure of the wooden hut provides an important juxtaposition with the figure of Alice's "wooden leg." The space in which these corpses reside is a place of lifelessness, and yet a particularly uncanny life inseparable from that of the dead appears before the eyes of the remaining victims. The relation between the dead bodies and the rats bears witness to the reality of dehumanization perpetrated by Hitler's Nazi Germany.

## ALICE'S LEG AS A MARKER OF LIFE AND OF DEATH

Caruth specifies that the crisis of fully knowing the event should not resist the concept that the delayed return of flashbacks or dreams are "absolutely *true* to the event."[32] The narrative thus suggests that the return of the leg signifies a repetition of the original trauma: "*Nous allions exprès voir si elle y était toujours et c'était chaque fois insoutenable*" ("We kept on going there to see if it was still there, and each time it was intolerable").[33] The presence of the leg brings back something unbearable about the death of the women's friend. Seeing the leg in this way means that the present and the ungrasped past are tied up with each other in one single moment.[34] These two different events are inextricably bound up with each other: "*Alice que nous ne pouvions approcher parce qu'une faiblesse nous clouait là. Alice qui mourait solitaire et n'appelait personne*" ("Alice we could not approach because weakness nailed us to the spot. Alice dying alone, not calling anyone").[35]

The temporal structure of this particular passage bears witness to the paradox of a trauma that originally happened at a different time and place. First, it describes the repeated return to Alice's leg that is experienced as intolerable. Second, it describes how Alice was left alone while the women were unable to approach her as she was dying in the snow. Alice's presence and absence are both marked by the remaining leg. The narrative uses the demonstrative pronoun *ce* (it) to show how the traumatic experience of Alice's dying interrupts the present moment. It becomes the locus of the trauma by defining the event "*c'était*" ("it was") as the most unbearable experience. This particular pronoun carries the immediacy of the past into the present in the very moment of seeing Alice's leg. The repetition again and again is unbearable. The women bear witness to the presence of a trauma that returns as a belated response to the overwhelming experience of seeing Alice's dying. Seeing Alice's leg as *lying* in the snow corresponds to the seeing of Alice as *dying* in the snow: no ordinary life and no ordinary death. The emergence of Alice's dying through the appearance of her leg brings up the catastrophic event of the past as a present intrusion of memory: "*Alice abandonnée qui mourait dans la neige. Alice que nous ne pouvions approcher parce qu'une faiblesse nous clouait là. Alice qui mourait solitaire et n'appelait personne*"[36] ("Alice abandoned, dying in the snow. Alice we could not approach because weakness nailed us to the spot. Alice dying alone, not calling anyone").[37]

Alice's leg holds a memory that flashes back as a traumatic history, calling the women in the present to an event that they never fully experienced. At the very core of this passage lies not only Alice's muteness but also the missed encounter with Alice's dying. If the women cannot experience Alice's dying, it is because her dying is timeless and infinite.[38] She is thus condemned to die an anonymous death, since there is no knowing of the precise moment of her death. The knowledge that the collective can claim is marked only by the process of Alice's dying and not by the moment at which her life ends, which continues to escape them. Alice's dying can thus be described as a crisis of knowing.

In this context, we understand that the women only *now*, by seeing Alice's leg, experience this overwhelming event. In the story of "The Same Day," Delbo describes that "*faiblesse*" ("weakness") kept the women from approaching Alice as she was dying, Alice's "not calling" remained as that which is unspeakable. Weakness constitutes the separation between Alice and the women and takes away the knowing of her death. The fact that Alice is "not calling" or is silent can be linked to the impossibility of approaching her. It is precisely the distance between Alice and the women that not only makes her dying impossible but also erases the possibility of a spoken exchange. Alice's dying becomes the space of a missed encounter that haunts all the women as a belated response to the unacceptable and incomprehensible event of leaving her behind.

The crisis of knowing is also a crisis within language.[39] The absence of calling—the break in language surrounding the dying of their friend—denies the women meaning. The return of the leg also brings with it the silent call that had originally received no answer. The impact of seeing Alice silently dying can also, therefore, be understood as a mute address calling for a voice to speak.

THE REAPPEARANCE OF THE LEG

Snow and mud play an important role in the continuous reappearance of Alice's leg. The geographical site where Alice's leg is found might be said to be the unconscious space that swallowed the experience until it returns repeatedly, and always, as an unexpected and surprising event. The seeing of the leg is described in terms of covering over and reappearing:

> *Alice était morte depuis des semaines que la jambe artificielle gisait encore sur la neige. Puis il a neigé de nouveau. La jambe a été recouverte. Elle a réapparu dans la boue. Cette jambe dans la boue. La jambe d'Alice—coupée vivante—dans la boue.*[40]

> Alice had been dead for weeks yet the artificial leg was still resting in the snow. Then it snowed again. The leg was covered over. It appeared in the mud. The leg in the mud. Alice's leg—severed alive—in the mud.

The rhythmic appearance and disappearance of Alice's leg signals the muddy reality of Alice's death, just as the traumatic image returns as a symptom of a traumatic history. In the same way that Alice's leg appears periodically from the snow in the mud, the traumatic experience comes back from a "timeless" unconscious space to "possess" the traumatized. Instead of seeing the leg as a stable visual object, the women are forced to see the leg whenever the weather conditions are such that the leg shows itself to them. It becomes clear that these specific changes of weather can be linked to the process of forgetting. In Freud's trauma studies, forgetting and remembering are inextricably linked. In her discussion on *the structure of experience* as it relates to Freud's concept, Caruth draws attention to amnesia experienced during the time of a traumatic event and the belated return of painful memories. In other words, the event stored in the unconscious returns unexpectedly and repeatedly without the subject's conscious decision to remember. The traumatized periodically remembers and forgets that which she has never experienced in the first place. It seems as if the women have to face the repeated return of the literality of the event. The attempt to grasp its meaning is interrupted by the changing conditions of seeing the leg. Each time the women see Alice's leg under different conditions, they experience Alice's dying again under different internal conditions.

The unspeakability of the event is visually marked in the last sentence of the passage by two lines representing two blanks. These two blanks can be read as the space of their traumatic experience that is inaccessible. The two lines establish a condition of the break within a coherent narrative.

THE DISAPPEARANCE OF THE LEG

Alice's leg disappears as mysteriously as it arrived. Delbo describes the disappearance of Alice's leg as a surprise: "*Un jour elle n'y était plus*" ("One day it was not there anymore").[41] Someone says that Alice's leg disappeared from one day to the next and that it is no longer in the same location. The unexpected departure of Alice's leg seems to correspond to the sudden arrival of it. For all the women, the loss of the leg disrupts the seeing of the leg: "*Nous l'avons vue longtemps*" ("We saw it a long time").[42] The grammatical sign of the French pronoun of place "*y*" ("*Un jour elle n'y était plus*") signifies a location. Here, the question of place is inseparable from that of the traumatic history. As we have seen earlier, the experience of returning to Alice's dying in the snow through seeing Alice's leg lying in the snow is placed within the structure of trauma. By reading the "*y*" in relation to trauma, "*y*" defines the place in which both the present and the past came together precisely at the point where Alice's leg first appeared. The disappearance of the leg suggests that there will be no way in which to return to that earlier moment and possess its full significance. In this sense, the disappearance of Alice's leg corresponds to both the brutality of Alice's dying and the impossibility of approaching her *in front of* Block 25. (Let us recall that all of the women were forced to stay *behind* Block 25). Delbo marks in language that the women are now unable to see both Alice and her leg: "*Elle n'y était plus*" ("One day it was not there anymore"). The personal pronoun "*elle*" (it) replaces the feminine nouns. Since both "*la jambe*" ("the leg") and "Alice" can be defined by the linguistic inscription of feminine gender, "*elle*" signals that Alice and her leg simultaneously remain lost. Losing the leg brings this community into a fundamental crisis.

The enigma of how Alice's leg disappeared seems to prompt a significant response that is without proof. To explain the mysterious loss, the women make up their own story telling that "someone" must have taken the leg to make a fire: "*Quelqu'un avait dû la prendre pour faire du feu*"

("Someone must have filched it to make a fire").[43] By saying that some-one else must have taken the leg away, the companions assert both the surprise of losing the leg and the impossibility of keeping the leg in their possession. Strangely enough, the women not only blame someone else for taking "their" leg away, but they also assume that this person must have made a fire with Alice's leg. In assuming that "someone" must have taken the leg away, the women presuppose that a single and yet un-known person removed the leg from its place and carried it to another place. More explicitly, the women link the enigmatic and sudden event of losing the leg to the making of a fire. It seems as if the leg, which once belonged to Alice's companions, had been eliminated by the destructive power of the fire. On the one hand, the significance of burning points to the fact that Alice's leg has been transformed from being alive and sen-tient back into being an ordinary piece of wood. On the other hand, burning the leg means it can no longer be located as a remnant of Alice. Alice's leg seems to have faded away: *"Nous l'avons vue longtemps"* ("We saw it a long time"). In not seeing the leg, the women sense that a trans-formation has taken place.

The burning of the leg is attributed to a gypsy woman: *"Une tzigane sûrement, personne autre n'aurait eu le courage"* ("A gypsy woman surely, no one else would have dared").[44] In saying that exclusively a gypsy woman could have burnt the leg, the women introduce another female—outside of their community—who is responsible for the act of burning.[45] If the women deploy for their story a gypsy woman as the one who carries out the act of burning, how do we understand the relation be-tween these women and a gypsy woman? The women attempt to differ-entiate themselves from the woman who burns the leg. Yet, it is signifi-cant to note that both the women and the gypsy woman have no common experience or "possession" of the leg. The indifference of the gypsy wom-an to the leg seems to underscore the other women's own inability to possess this memory or the original experience it signifies. Not only do the women not consciously experience the sudden loss of the leg, they do not even experience the making of their own story. Rather, they want their own story to be taken for a reality to understand the disappearance of the leg. To say that *"Quelqu'un avait dû la prendre pour faire du feu. Une tzigane sûrement, personne autre n'aurait eu le courage"* ("Someone must have filched it to make a fire. A gypsy woman surely, no one else would have dared")[46] is not simply a matter of not knowing nor is it a matter of proof. It means that the experience of losing the leg presupposes another event unknowable to all of them. While they assume or reassure them-selves that they know, the women produce a new meaning that is exclu-sively linked to a gypsy woman. If the gypsy woman is the link between the women and the disappearance of the leg, what is the function of the gypsy woman in the act of burning the leg?

The disappearance of the leg through the indifferent act of the gypsy woman represents a form of forgetting that overtakes all of the women. It appears within the narrative as a powerful act that is bound up with the figure of a gypsy and the figure of fire.[47] Since the gypsy woman is not engaged in the seeing of the leg but in the burning of it, she appears to figure the act of forgetting. Her burning of the leg signifies her action as something beyond the control of the other women.

If the leg disappears from the women's sight, however, it is not entirely consigned to oblivion. The story itself constitutes another reappearance of the leg, no longer as a traumatic vision but as the trace of this experience in the form of Delbo's own testimonial narrative. It is ultimately the story, indeed, that will become the site of the leg's incessant return.

THE WRITING OF ALICE'S LEG

Delbo's story must thus be read in terms of its own role in returning the leg to sight and memory. Her writing makes Alice alive by marking her dying as that which in itself can never be present. The process of "marking" a presence is at the same time the marking of an absence: Alice's dying. But this marking also provides a trace of the event that refuses to be erased. In *Of Grammatology* (1976), Jacques Derrida introduces the concept of the supplement in relation to writing as a prosthetic device. For him, the supplement "signifies nothing, simply replaces a lack."[48] He argues that: "the supplement is neither a presence nor an absence.[49] According to Derrida:

> But the supplement supplements. It adds only to replace.
> It intervenes or insinuates itself *in-the-place-of*; if it fills,
> it is as if one fills a void. If it represents and makes an image,
> it is by the anterior default of a presence. Compensatory [*suppléant*]
> and vicarious, the supplement is an adjunct, a subaltern instance
> which *takes* (the) *place* [*tient lieu*].[50]

Influenced by Derrida's work and theory on the supplement, David Wills wrote his remarkable book *Prosthesis* in which he narrates the story of his father's amputated leg and the writing about it. Wills engages in the concept of prosthesis as a corporeal and literary supplement, giving significance to the uncanny wooden leg and the son's memory of seeing his father's distress with an artificial device.[51] For him: "Prosthesis arises of two putatively distinct orders such as literal/figurative, nature/artifice or theory/fiction."[52] But it is also the distinction between his father's actual "prosthesis" (a wooden leg) and *"Prosthesis"* (his own writing). What determines the notion of Prosthesis is the uneasy combination of two different discourses such as "the wooden leg and all the returning phantoms that work through it."[53] Wills insists: "It [prosthesis] embarks instead upon the production of its own literary artifact in the form of a fragmentary and episodic story of a father's wooden leg."[54] To follow Will's point, I wish to highlight the correspondence between Alice's wooden leg as a prosthetic device and Delbo's Prosthesis as a supplementary writing of Alice's dying.

Delbo's figurative writing of Alice's Leg suggests a profound resonance between Derrida's concept of supplement and Wills's supplemental division between "prosthesis" and *Prosthesis*. As a peculiar metonymy for Alice, I argue, Alice's leg functions also as a prosthetic writing that supplements for her absence and her story that can never be told. Like Alice's leg, which becomes alive through the return of the traumatic experience, the story of Alice's leg becomes alive through the writing *of* it.

In the case of Delbo's story "Alice's Leg," the figure of a "wooden leg," holds an account of Alice's cruel death. Wills identifies the composition of *Prosthesis* as "generalized prosthetization meaning that the wooden leg, together with all the returning phantoms that work through it . . . making it an uneasy combination of different discourses."[55] In Delbo, it is precisely the relation between the text of "Alice's leg" and the pain that derives from seeing an anonymous wooden leg that mark the composition of *Prosthesis*. Knowing about Alice's dying depends upon the artificial device of the figure of Alice's Leg. In other words, the traumatic experience of the women in relation to Alice's death is embarked upon in Delbo's literary artifact in the form of a fragmentary and episodic story of Alice's wooden leg. Alice's leg, indeed, functions not only as a metonymy within the narrative but also as a marker that stands in for the original experience that the narrative cannot relate. The leg within the story— which functions as a prosthesis—thus becomes a figure that has a prosthetic function within the text. The painful experience of seeing Alice's dying thus becomes the origin of writing. The writing of Alice's leg does not transmit knowledge of the death but something more like its written afterlife. Writing of Alice's absence through the figure of a leg marks her death without knowing that the marking of her death has occurred. Paradoxically, it is precisely Alice's death that is signified through this particular wooden leg. Alice's leg appears as a figure to inscribe the painful experience of Alice's dying and the disappearance of her body in the anonymity of death.

In this sense, Delbo's text could be said to be a figurative, or literary, testimony of the Holocaust, a text that passes on through figures what cannot be conveyed in literal terms. The terms must remain figurative, in this text, because there are no literal terms that can name this event. As we recall, the women suffer the impossibility of approaching Alice, who stays silent for them. Writing can also be seen as the marking of that which can never be reached, but we can read the inhuman silencing of the event through the figure of Alice's leg. How, then, are we going to approach Alice's leg as a testimony of the Holocaust? It is precisely the

story of Alice's leg that signifies the difficulty of remembering and bringing testimony to the event of the Holocaust. Can there be a seeing if
Alice's leg marks that which cannot be seen? How do we read Alice's leg
on the level of language?

In the context of Delbo's testimony, her obligation to make readers see
["*Il faut donner à voir*"] became the motivating force for writing the literary memoirs. Critics have pointed out the survivor's central concern is
linked to the experiences of female prisoners. However, there is no important distinction that seems to be associated with her gendered writing.
According to Myrna Goldenberg and Amy H. Shapiro's arguments in
their important edited volume *Different Horrors/Same Hell*, scholars have
only recently engaged with feminist theoretical analyses of gender. In
addition, both feminist scholars point out that academics lack a critical
examination of their own gender assumptions.[56] For example, Federica
K. Clementi's critical book *Holocaust Mothers & Daughters, Family History,
and Trauma*, prompts us to engage in the presence of women in Holocaust
literature. In her study, she cites the work of many American feminist
scholars such as Marianne Hirsch who have engaged in the reformula-
tions of the maternal figure in our culture.[57] In terms of the early feminist
movement, critic and Holocaust scholar Susan Rubin Suleiman was
among the first theorists to draw attention to the feminine marginaliza-
tion, particularly the conjunction of writing and motherhood. In her essay, "Writing and Motherhood" (1979), she presents readers with her
self-addressed question: "Why did I choose to write about writing and
motherhood?" to highlight the exclusion of mothers from the scene of
feminine writing within a male dominated society.[58] Suleiman traces the
psychoanalytical view of motherhood in the traditional literature claiming that Freud's writing on motherhood emerges out of his own sexism.
To exemplify the theme of writing and artistic relation as it pertains to
mothers, Suleiman cites Helene Deutsch's quote: *Mothers don't write, they
are written*, which exemplifies "the underlying assumption of most
psychoanalytic theories."[59] In this context, Suleiman refers to the works
of three prominent French feminist theorists, Julia Kristeva, Luce Irigaray, and Hélène Cixous and to their work on motherhood, which "insisted on the essentially subversive, disorderly nature of women's writing, without differentiating between the feminine and the maternal."[60] In
the context of the French feminist theory, in particular the concept of
*l'écriture féminine*, Hélène Cixous argues that being a woman means that
one is "never far from the 'mother,'" claiming that the notion of "other"
emerges within the mother's force of "reparation and nourishment" and
therefore stands in relation to "desiccated rationalism of male discourse."[61] As this statement shows, Cixous provides a link between self
and m/other and does not differentiate between feminine and maternal.
This theory of a Jewish writer inspires me to propose Delbo's alternative
form of motherhood intrinsic in her writing.

Despite the fact that Delbo was not a mother, her writing embodies a maternal function, a maternal function of nourishment. Contrary to the self-constituting subjectivity inscribed in feminine discourse, her attempt to bring the stories of female victims to life and putting them first, symbolically elevates Delbo's writing to that of a maternal figure. Even though Delbo's act of writing cannot be compared with the fate of Jewish mothers who entered the concentration camps and were automatically selected for the gas chambers, her sense of nourishing the remembrance of the victims can be linked to that of a maternal function. In so doing, Delbo makes visible her investment in a life of vibrant remembrance amidst death. In the specific historical event of "Alice's Leg," Delbo depicts the destruction of a female body. While facing Alice dying and returning to the traumatic event by seeing a wooden leg in front of Block 25, in the aftermath of her imprisonment, Delbo creates a textual prosthesis to create a life for Alice after her death. Likewise, in "Alice's Leg," she writes against the devaluated position of women by a woman in the concentration camps from within a sadistic-patriarchal-society.

## SEEING AS AN ACT OF READING

In conclusion, Alice's leg is a literary device that can be seen as a figure that unfolds through the process of reading. For a reader, the process of seeing is inextricably bound up with reading. In the reading of "Alice's Leg," the figure points both to and away from the original event. This suggests both the impossibility of grasping the original event and the impossibility to return to a single meaning. Although the leg remains in its singular or material form, the process of reading allows us multiple ways to bring the memory of Alice into the future. Whether or not—and how—we perceive Alice's leg in the process of reading depends upon our own condition of reading that is inextricably linked with the experience of reading such a traumatic history.[62]

The story and its central figure continue to speak to us of an experience that will never be present to us. The text thus calls on the reader to interpret and discover a truth that remains elusive and yet imperative to recall. Each reading demands a new encounter and a new attempt to read and discover what simply cannot be known. As readers, we are called by Alice's leg for a reading that might change each time we return to the scene of reading that refers beyond the single story of Alice. The story, indeed, extends beyond the violent act that was imposed upon Alice, and speaks to the experiences of all victims of the Holocaust. Alice's leg cannot appear in the space of one single meaning, and refuses to close off, within a single meaning, the significance of the Holocaust.

The leg, as a figure, imposes itself upon us with the force of Simone's simple imperative: *"Venez voir."* This is a call for our participation in the process of Alice's dying, since Alice cannot speak for herself anymore. It is precisely her leg as a prosthesis that calls to us as a result of her specific way of dying. Alice's encounter with death and the anonymous disappearance of her body within the masses of bodies remains as something that can never be identified. Instead, it is her leg that designates the imperative of reading, through which meaning can be produced. It is the silence of the leg—lying in the figurative dimension of language—that calls all of us to come and see.

## NOTES

1. Charlotte Delbo, *Auschwitz and After*, trans Rosette C. Lamont, introd. Lawrence L. Langer (New Haven and London: Yale University Press, 1995), vii. Lamont recalls Delbo's repetitive avowal to transmit the knowledge she acquired in *l'univers concentrationionnaire*.

2. Nicole Thatcher, *A Literary Analysis of Charlotte Delbo's Concentration Camp Re-Presentation* (Lewiston, NY: Edwin Mellen Press, 1999), 54.

3. Louis Jouvet (1881–1951) was a renowned French actor, director, and theater director.

4. For more detailed biographical information, see Charlotte Delbo, *Le convoi du 24 Janvier* (Paris: Minuit, 1965); *Convoy to Auschwitz: Women of the French Resistance*, trans. Carol Cosman (Boston: Northeastern University Press, 1997).

5. Charlotte Delbo, *Aucun de nous ne reviendra*, hereafter referred to as *AR*. Published in English as "None of Us Will Return," in *Auschwitz and After*, 35–40, hereafter referred to as *AA*.

6. Charlotte Delbo, *AA*, 19.

7. Michael Rothberg, *Traumatic Realism: The Demands of Holocaust Representations* (Minneapolis and London: University of Minnesota Press, 2000), 139.

8. Ibid., 142.

9. Karein K. Goertz, "Body, Trauma, and the Rituals of Memory: Charlotte Delbo and Ruth Klüger," in *Shaping Losses: Cultural Memory and the Holocaust*, eds. Julia Epstein and Lori Hope Lefkovitz (Urbana and Chicago: University of Illinois Press, 2001), 178.

10. Charlotte Delbo, *AA*, xi.

11. Charlotte Delbo, "La jambe d'Alice," 67.

12. Charlotte Delbo, "Le même jour" in *Aucun de nous ne reviendra*, 58–66. Published in English as "The Same Day," in *Auschwitz and After*, 35–40.

13. Michael S. Roth, *Memory, Trauma and History: Essays on Living with the Past* (New York: Columbia University Press, 2011), 78. In the twentieth century, or the "century of Testimony," critical debates regarding the relationship between trauma and language, as they relate to survivors' historical literary testimonies, have been widespread across the humanities. Much of the work on trauma in relation to Holocaust testimonies stems from the period in the late 1980s when the American Psychiatric Association acknowledged the term "post-traumatic stress disorder" to understand the impact of trauma on the psyche of victims who had experienced an overwhelming catastrophic event. Scholarly criticism, in particular in the fields of literary studies, history, and cultural studies, turned to the problematic relation between experience and representation within the narratives of survivors.

14. Cathy Caruth, ed., *Trauma: Explorations in Memory* (Baltimore: Johns Hopkins University Press, 1995), 3–11.

15. Caruth, 5. In contrast to Caruth's close reading of Freud's 1920 text, Ruth Leys's *Trauma: A Genealogy* (Chicago: University of Chicago Press, 2000), provides a historical genealogy of trauma. Leys repudiates Caruth's poststructuralist work on trauma, in

particular her failure to differentiate between literature and history. Karyn Ball, *Disciplining the Holocaust* (Albany: State University of New York, 2009) cites Leys's critical response to Caruth's idea on the notion of the "literality of the event," claiming that the event leaves behind a material registration that is "dissociated from normal mental processes of cognition," and that these belated flashbacks stand "outside representation." See also, Michael André Bernstein, *Forgone Conclusions: Against Apocalyptic History* (Berkeley, Los Angeles, and London: University of California Press, 1994).

16. Charlotte Delbo, "Le même jour" in *Aucun de nous ne reviendra*, 58–66. Published in English as "The Same Day," in *Auschwitz and After*, 35–40.

17. Charlotte Delbo, *AR*, 59.

18. Charlotte Delbo, *AA*, 35.

19. Charlotte Delbo, *AR*, 60-61.

20. Charlotte Delbo, *AA*, 36.

21. Delbo, *AA*, 41; Delbo, *AR*, 63.

22. Delbo, *AA*, 39; Delbo, *AR*, 67.

23. Stewart Veronica, "Reading Trauma: Charlotte Delbo and the Struggle to Represent," in *Between the Psyche and the Polis: Refiguring History in Literature and Theory*, ed. Michael Rossington and Anne Whitehead (Aldershot, UK: Ashgate, 2001), 97–107.

24. Delbo, *AA*, 40; Delbo, *AR*, 66.

25. Caruth, *Trauma*, 4–5.

26. Caruth, *Trauma*, 9.

27. Delbo, *AA*, 41; Delbo, *AR*, 67.

28. Delbo, *AA*, 41; Delbo, *AR*, 67.

29. Delbo, *AA*, 41; Delbo, *AR*, 68.

30. Delbo, *AA*, 41; Delbo, *AR*, 68.

31. See *Dictionary of Medical Terms*, 4th edition, (London: Bloomsburg Publishers, 2004). The electronic edition was published in 2011. See also David Wills, *Prosthesis* (Stanford: Stanford University Press, 1995), 247–49. Wills traces the historical definition between the rhetorical and medical use of the term prosthesis.

32. Caruth, *Trauma*, 5.

33. Delbo, *AA*, 41; *AR*, 67.

34. Caruth, *Trauma*, 5.

35. Delbo, *AA*, 41; *AR*, 68.

36. Delbo, *AR*, 68.

37. Delbo, *AA*, 41.

38. In his argument about trauma in *Beyond the Pleasure Principle*, Freud describes that "unconscious" mental processes are in and of themselves "timeless" (31). It is the nature of trauma that is intimately bound up with the endless dying of Alice because trauma forces the women to insistently return to the seeing of Alice's fall and dying in the snow.

39. See Caruth's insightful chapters on the question of trauma and the language of literature in Cathy Caruth, *Unclaimed Experience: Trauma, Narrative, and History* (Baltimore and London: Johns Hopkins University Press, 1996).

40. Delbo, *AA*, 41; Delbo, *AR*, 68.

41. Delbo, *AA*, 41; Delbo, *AR*, 68.

42. Delbo, *AA*, 41; Delbo, *AR*, 68.

43. Maurice Blanchot, *The Infinite Conversation*, trans. Lydia Davis (Minneapolis: University of Minnesota Press, 1992), 379–85. Blanchot explains that a narrative is a forgetting. "It is narrative (independent of its content) that is a forgetting, so that to tell a story is to put oneself through the ordeal of this first forgetting that precedes, founds, and ruins all memory. Recounting, in this sense, is the torment of language."

44. Delbo, *AA*, 41; Delbo, *AR*, 68.

45. On questions of community see Thomas Trezise, "The Question of Community in Charlotte Delbo's 'Auschwitz and After,'" *MLN* 117 (2002): 858–85.

46. Delbo, *AA*, 41.

47. In "Forgetful Memory," Blanchot does not identify the power of forgetting with the negative. Rather he points to the fact that the very power of forgetting opens up a neutral space: "There is in memory a relation we can no longer term dialectical, since it belongs to the ambiguity of forgetting that is at once the mediating site and a space without mediation—indifferent difference between depth and surface; as though to forget were always to forget profoundly, but also as though the depth of forgetting were profound only by the forgetting of all depth." See Blanchot, *Infinite Conversation*, 316–17.

48. Jacques Derrida, *Of Grammatology*, trans. Gayatri Chakravorty Spivak (Baltimore and London: Johns Hopkins University Press, 1974), 208.

49. Ibid., 314. The supplement represents not only the act of writing but also the precarious relationship between terms like "speech" and "writing," which he argues should not be stacked in a hierarchy, but rather viewed as supplementing one another.

50. Ibid., 145.

51. David Wills, *Prosthesis*, Meridian: Crossing Aesthetics (Stanford: Stanford University Press, 1995), 10.

52. Ibid., 10.

53. Ibid., 10.

54. Ibid., 11.

55. Ibid., 10.

56. Myrna Goldenberg and Amy H. Shapiro, eds., *Different Horrors, Same Hell: Gender and The Holocaust* (Seattle and London: University of Washington Press, 2013), 4.

57. Federica K. Clementi, *Holocaust Mothers & Daughters: Family, History, and Trauma* (Waltham, Massachusetts: Brandeis University Press, 2013), 11. See especially Marianne Hirsch's influential work *The Mother/Daughter Plot: Narrative, Psychoanalysis, Feminism* (Bloomington: Indiana University Press, 1989) in which she particularly focuses on motherhood and the complex mother/daughter relationship within literary representations.

58. Susan Rubin Suleiman, "Writing Motherhood" in *Mother Reader: Essential Writings on Motherhood*, ed. Moyra Davey (New York, London, Toronto, and Sydney: Seven Stories Press, 1979), 114.

59. Susan Rubin Suleiman, "Writing Motherhood," in *Mother Reader: Essential Writings on Motherhood*, ed. by Moyra Davey (New York. London. Toronto & Sydney: Seven Stories Press, 1979), 115.

60. Suleiman, 117.

61. Ibid., 128.

62. Thomas Trezise, "The Question of Community in Charlotte Delbo's *Auschwitz and After*," *MLN* 117, no. 4 (September 2002): 858–66. Trezise examines Delbo's literary testimonial work. In reading the survivor's trilogy of memoirs, he addresses Delbo's fragmentary language in relation to trauma and survival. In particular, Trezise proposes that the first-person pronoun "us" recurring in the title of the first volume *None of us will return* raises the question of community both during and after Auschwitz. Questioning to whom the pronoun "us" refers, he claims that the pronoun "us" (or "we) does not always designates Delbo's community of female inmates but that it can also mean all the groups male and female imprisoned in Birkenau and the "concentrationary universe" in its entirety and that the community could be arguably be extended to all those deported to labor, concentration and death camps, not to forget the groups that suffered the pre-Holocaust Nazi's threat. Pertinent to the question of community was also the Nazi strategy to differentiate between non-Jewish and Jewish women including the ambiguity of the word "return." Binding the notion of community to the word "return," Tresize proposes that a return of "us" is not linked to a biological return of the survivors but also to the spectral presence of the dead in the testimonies of survivors. In emphasizing Delbo's motivation to bear witness "*Il faut donner à voir*," Tresize points out that Delbo's use of the pronoun "us" also relates to the responses post-Holocaust public community who might be haunted by "a past that will not pass."

# FOUR

## Embodied Existence of Mothers

### Gisella Perl and Olga Lengyel

Olga Lengyel and Gisella Perl—both survivors of the concentration camp Auschwitz-Birkenau—were among the first female victims who published their memoirs shortly after liberation: Olga Lengyel, *Five Chimneys. A Woman Survivor's True Story of Auschwitz*,[1] and Gisella Perl, *I was a Doctor in Auschwitz*.[2] At a time when little attention was given to gender studies, both women concentrate primarily upon female victims. Committed to giving testimony to the Nazi atrocities, both authors narrate personal, individual, and collective experiences, thereby documenting the systematic torture imposed upon the female body, in particular pregnant women and their unborn babies. In the years following the war, these important first person stories remained on the margins of a vast Holocaust research. Despite the important work of the two women, it took forty-eight years for Lengyel's *Five Chimneys* (1995) and thirty-one years for Perl's *I was a Doctor in Auschwitz* (1979) to be republished.

Sarah R. Horowitz, one of the early pioneer's examining Shoah narratives from the perspective of gender, argues that women's experiences are significantly different from those of male survivors:

> Missing from male versions of survival are experiences unique to women such as menarche, menstruation and pregnancy in the concentration camps; the strategies some women devised to endure and survive, the ways other women met their deaths; the subsequent effect on women survivors, in family, friendship, and civic relations, and the way women reconstruct shattered paradigms of meaning in the face of cultural and personal displacements.[3]

In the context of her statement that "women may remember differently from men, or they may remember different things," these two poignant memoirs testify to the incredible courage of two Jewish women to save lives in the midst of death.[4] Bolstering Horowitz's argument, Lengyel and Perl write about women's enforced labor as doctors in the camps' hospital. Their accounts revolve solely around female experiences, and demonstrate the ways in which the two survivors remember and recount their unique experiences differently from the male victims. In her article, "Gender and Family Studies," Judith Tydor Baumel investigates early memoirs of women survivors.[5] Examining specific characteristics of these first female writings, she argues that these written memoirs are characterized by their authenticity and that memory had not yet been blurred by the passage of time. These writings are devoid of moral preaching, while they concentrate on women's experiences such as rape and childbirth, they did so at a time when it was uncommon to conceptualize the role of gender in testimonies of trauma, and therefore they maintain their authenticity as first person, eyewitness accounts. In addition, she points out that female authors only wrote briefly about their prewar life and that most male authors wrote several pages to account for their prewar and interwar experiences. Particularly, she emphasizes the distinct role of female self-help and mutual support in contributing to the authors' experiences in the camps and their survival.

This chapter investigates Lengyel and Perl's accounts of the horrifying experiments imposed upon the female body and how the body itself becomes an object of amusement and extreme torture tied to SS sadism. What is at stake here is the arbitrary viciousness of the perpetrators to harm and dehumanize the female victims, and particularly to annihilate Jewish women, mothers, and children. In the attempt to save the lives of female victims, in particular mothers, Perl and Lengyel recall in detail the degrading atrocities committed upon *female bodies*. Both survivors write from their gendered perspectives, thus producing a reconstructed, yet still fragmented body of women's writing. Questions related to female nakedness, pregnancy, and killing of newborns demand the readers' attention and call for an ethics of female remembrance.

## My Number Tells I was "There"

"I was number 25403. I still have it on my right arm and shall carry it with me to my grave," remembers Olga Lengyel in her autobiographical narrative.[6] *Five Chimneys* is one of the most detailed eyewitness accounts of the Nazis' methodological techniques of systematic torture and annihilation of women, Jews, and non-Jews. Lengyel turns her experience into a story that inverts the useless suffering of individual lives into a living remembrance. She writes about her prewar family life, the unforeseen journey to Auschwitz, her experiences as an inmate, and her work as a nurse in the infirmary of Auschwitz-Birkenau. Each of the twenty-three narrative chapters provides an insight into the immediate circumstances after arrival at the camps—such as being sent "to the left side" for direct extermination, or to the right to become a cog in the incessant machinery of destruction devised to break the victims before being gassed and burned in the crematory ovens. Perl's distinct language communicates the terrifying situations. Each chapter of her testimony describes the selective processes of destruction and the complexities of survival. Perl's twenty-three chapters illustrate the intersections between life and death by detailing the power of the perpetrators' deliberate destruction of women's bodies. Alongside her description of the journey in the cattle car, the arrival in the camps, the selections, the roll call, life in Barrack 26, work in the infirmary, the method and the madness, sexual activities in the camps, or the march to liberation, she plunges the reader into the details of the camp organization and the treatment of the inmates. Lengyel bears witness to life-threatening experiences of the female victims in the name of medical care and scientific experiments under the SS physicians Dr. Fritz Klein and the chief-physician Dr. Josef Mengele. Describing the beautiful and sadistic "blond angel" Irma Griese who was the head of the women's camp, the survivor-writer remembers, "The moral terror which her mere presence inspired visibly pleased her. For this twenty-two-year-old girl was completely without pity."[7] This sentence recalls the physical and emotional sensations the author experienced when exposed to the arbitrary yet extreme oppression and subordination of an evil woman.

A fuller understanding of these testimonies emerges when reading these works through the lens of gender theory in the field of Holocaust studies. In the last thirty-five years, this approach has become central to many of the debates about women's experiences and the Holocaust.[8] Joan Ringelheim, a leading pioneer in this field, shed light on the study of Jewish women, gender, and sexuality in her important essay: "Woman and the Holocaust: A Reconsideration of Research" (1985). Ringelheim asks, "In what ways did sexism function in the racist ideology against Jews and other so called non-Aryans?" in order to underscore the critical lack of women's experiences in the discourse of Holocaust Studies in the 1980s.[9] Early important works of feminist scholars such as Myrna Goldenberg, Doris L. Bergen, Marianne Hirsch, Marion Kaplan, S. Lillian Kremer, Claudia Konz, Vera Laska, Carol Ritter, John Roth, Sara R. Horowitz, Dalia Ofer, and Leonore J. Weitzman have become indispensable sources in the field of Gender Studies and the Holocaust.[10] The recent works of Sonja Maria Hedgepeth and Rochelle G. Saidel, *Sexual Violence against Jewish Women During the Holocaust* (2010), Myrna Goldenberg and Amy H. Shapiro's *Different Horrors, Same Hell: Gender and the Holocaust* (2012), Wendy Lower's *Hitler's Furies: German Women in the Nazi Fields* (2013), and Federica K. Clementi's book *Holocaust Mothers & Daughters: Family, History, and Trauma* (2013) are remarkable studies essential to interdisciplinary Gender Studies and the Holocaust.[11] Building on the work of these important scholars, I turn my attention to how Lengyel and Perl construct female/gender specific memories of personal, individual, and collective experiences in order to recoup their testimonies and authorial voices as well as the distinct positions of female victims of the Holocaust. The testimonies may remain fragmented, but female bodies are now wholly recognized and acknowledged alongside a body of writing that bears witness to the unique experiences of female victims and perpetrators.

THE STRIPPING APART OF AN EASTERN
EUROPEAN JEWISH FAMILY

Lengyel sets up her memoir in such a way to make the reader understand the systematic destruction of Jewish family life. These lives were arbitrarily abolished by the SS troops who ordered the transport of Jews of all ages to the concentration camps. The survivor dedicates the first chapter of her memoir, "8 Horses—or 96 Men, Women, and Children" to her dead family who were immediately sent to the gas chambers after arriving in Auschwitz. To understand the Nazi assault on Jewish communities, it is important to highlight the destruction of Lengyel's family. Lengyel tells us that the household of seven people lived in Cluj, the capital of Transylvania that formerly belonged to Romania but came under Hungarian control in 1940.[12] Knowing that "The Germans were the masters," the family wanted to accommodate their fear by going about the daily tasks "nay, we prayed—that the day of reckoning was not too far off."[13] Lengyel's husband Miklós was the director of his own hospital that the family had built in 1937. Specialized in general surgery and gynecology, Olga's training as a surgical assistant allowed her to be her husband's first assistant. The couple was devoted to their two sons Thomas and Arvad and enjoyed living with Olga's parents and her godfather, Professor Elfer Aladar, a famous internist.[14]

In her memoir, she remembers the devastating story of how her husband was falsely accused "of boycotting the use of German pharmaceutical preparation in the clinic."[15] Repeatedly interrogated by the members of the SS, he was deported within hours of his interrogation. Unaware of what was about to come, Lengyel decided to follow her husband instead of remaining in Cluj and being separated from him. As a result, the entire family decided to leave Cluj in order to stay together. Lengyel remembers the shock of understanding that they were all now victims of the Germans' nasty technique to draw whole families to the train station to transport them in cattle cars to the concentration camps. Remembering their deportation, Lengyel made clear that she underestimated the ugly manipulation of the "feared SS," and the impossibility of escaping the trans-

portation to Auschwitz-Birkenau.[16] At one point, Lengyel
at the end of the seventh day, the death car halted. We h
where? Was this a city? And what would they do to us
narrative, this mother of two sons describes one of her most pu
riences: the death of her son Arvad who was immediately sent off to the
gas chambers due to her honesty vis-à-vis a Nazi doctor. Dr. Fritz Klein
assumed that he was over twelve years old, but she truthfully answered
that he was not quite twelve years old yet. Immediately, he was sent off
to the left side, which meant that he was gassed with his younger brother
Thomas and their grandmother.[18]

HUMILIATION: NAKEDNESS IN THE CONCENTRATION CAMPS

Documenting the vulnerability of Jewish victims was one of the most
enjoyable tasks of the bestial Nazi perpetrators in their plots of systematic
destruction of European Jewry. Despite their gender differences, men
and women had to suffer the horrendous brutality of the torturers. Myrna Goldenberg and Amy H. Shapiro's expression "Different Horrors,
Same Hell" not only refers to the experiences of dehumanization but also
encourages researchers to differentiate between the male and female experience.[19] Among the most familiar images published after the war are
those that expose the victims in their nakedness. The exposure of the
victims' nakedness marks the Nazi's methodology to strip innocent people—men and women—of any kind of humanity. The practices of the
perpetrators that forced women to be exposed to the gaze of the SS
guards are central to Lengyel's narrative. In contrast to the actual situation of the victim's physical nakedness, I emphasize the concept of nakedness in the arts in order to underscore the Nazis' violation of human
dignity.

Representations of nude female and male figures in relation to the
unclothed body have been the subject of Western art throughout centu-
ries. In *Ways of Seeing*, John Berger, an English art critic, calls attention to
the distinction between nakedness and nudity in the tradition of painting.[20] In his influential text on art criticism, he writes, "To be naked is to
be oneself. To be nude is to be seen naked by others and yet not recognized for oneself."[21] In discussing what is involved in seeing, Berger
claims a naked body has to become objectified in order to become a nude.
In other words, nakedness reveals itself and nudity is placed on display.
In conceptualizing the aesthetic image of an "undressed" female body, he
argues that "nakedness" is not, however, an expression of her own
[woman] feelings; it is a sign of her [woman] submission to the owner's
feelings or demands" (the owner and painting).[22] In *Existence & Existents*,
Emmanuel Levinas states that the ones we encounter in society are
clothed beings. He argues, "in the world the other is an object already

trough his clothing."[23] Nakedness is that which one would like to hide from others but also from oneself, one's inescapable attachment to being or the scandal of the brute presence of one's being to itself. Nudity is a personal affair because one exposes the body to another.

## PROPAGATING DEHUMANIZATION AND OBJECTIFICATION OF FEMALE BODIES

At issue are dehumanization, humiliation, and sex-based violence. In her article on Holocaust films, Sybil Milton claims that nudity and naked corpses "are not to evoke a macabre sense of sadistic sex," but that nudity in the context of "selection" was part of the Nazis systematic destructive degradation before intimidating the victims prior to annihilation.[24] As the following episodes show, the female victims had to subordinate their bodies to the dominance and the arbitrariness of female and male SS guards. Lengyel testifies to the barbaric treatment she experienced after arriving at the death camps. The terror and hate of the Nazi perpetrators against Jewish women is described in the following scene, "They struck our naked bodies with their truncheons, as we had seen the women doing a short time before to those wretched inmates."[25] As this quote shows, the inhuman treatment of the guards shows how the collective of women were under constant scrutiny of the perpetrators. Further, Lengyel remembers how drunken soldiers ordered the women to strip off their clothes and leave behind all private items: "Undress! Leave all your clothing here. Leave your papers, valuables, medical equipment; and form rows against the wall."[26] This command attests to the Nazi methodology of manipulating the distinction between domination and subordination. Leaving the victims with nothing other than their naked body shows that the generated systematic destruction has taken ownership of all women who enter the gate of death.

## THE ASSAULTS ON THE FEMALE BODY

Lengyel describes a situation that reveals the bestial power of the perpetrators to expose the defenseless prisoners in a position of complete vulnerability and sexual humiliation. The relation between the Nazi ideology and their imprisoned female victims becomes apparent in the following scene.

> Now we were compelled to undergo a thorough examination in the Nazi manner, oral, rectal, and vaginal—another horrible experience. We had to lie across the table, stark naked while they probed. All this in the presence of drunken soldiers who sat around the table, chuckling obscenely.[27]

Subjugated to the Nazi guards' examinations and possible cavity searches for hidden valuables, the writer-survivor's narrative makes visible how the women could not escape the perpetrators' intrusions enacted as a rape of one's subjectivity and intimate female identity. Essential to her victim's experience is the sexual human humiliation in relation to the diabolic sadism of the soldiers gazing at female bodies while using licentious sexist language. This horrible image questions the very foundation of human individuality and gender boundaries. If Hitler's ideology was solely based on anti-Semitism and his desire to annihilate the Jewish people, how can one understand the relation between the powerless naked victims at the hands of the drunken soldiers dominating these objectified women?[28] Reading Lengyel's episodes in relation to the patriarchal system of National Socialism and Nazi ideology, in particular the importance of manliness as a national symbol, the status of the nudity of female bodies is used to promote Nazi crimes. The female bodies become Nazi property, and serve to legitimate their heinous acts.

In fact, within the framework of the concentration camp, the female bodies are owned by the Nazi regime for the purpose of annihilation. The enforced state of "nakedness" in relation to the naked female bodies is a form of possession. The female body becomes subject to display and public denouncement in a space from which there is no escape; the nakedness of the women embodies their body as an object of destruction to the perpetrator's gaze.

George L. Mosse's relevant chapter "The New Fascist Man," is dedicated to the central role of modern masculinity in all fascist systems, "Fascism used manliness both as an ideal and in a practical manner in order to strengthen its political structure, but devotion to a higher cause was at the center of its concept of masculinity."[29] Mosse notes that the movement between nationalism and racism (the Nuremberg Race Laws) was the driving force behind creating the new fascist man.[30]

For the purpose of reading the nudity of the women's bodies displayed as an owned object to the perpetrators in the death camps, I wish to undermine the National Socialists' idea of masculinity both as imperative to build the "Aryan" nation and to plot the destruction against the Jewish people. Mosse sums up the obsession with the male body and its new meaning: "When the Third Reich was established, the male body had never before been elevated so self-consciously into a central political symbol."[31] According to him, Hitler's idea of manliness, advocated in *Mein Kampf*, was exemplified in the Greek ideal of beauty representing a healthy body and mind.[32] In addition, heroic and true manliness of an "Ideal Aryan" was not only expressed through the human body but depended also on sacrificing a family life for the higher cause of the "fatherland."[33] An example of male dominance within the Nazi system is the fact that women were subordinated to men and solely characterized as the procreator and the mother of her people.[34]

In contrast to the enforced uncanny spectacle of displaying the nude bodies of the women stands male nudity as a symbolic representation of the "Ideal Aryan." Mosse claims that "Men's bodies in their well-sculptured nudity became fascist symbols; women, with some exceptions such as the one just mentioned, kept their bodies at least partly clothed."[35] As we can see, the main objective of male nudity was to show the sculptured physical body featuring a new masculinity that stands in opposition to the bodies of the racial enemies, especially their primary opponent, the Jewish people.

MALE CAMARADERIE TO DEHUMANIZE THE FEMALE VICTIMS

Camaraderie takes on a new meaning within the Nationalist Socialist's formation of the "Männerbund." The bonding of men was one of the virtues of the "new fascist man" emphasizing "a camaraderie of males [that] was considered the foundation upon which the state rested."[36] Yet, Heinrich Himmler, Reichsführer of the SS, strictly opposed an erotically charged friendship between men.[37]

In this vein, the laughter of the soldiers who are standing together using obscene language to denounce the naked women recalls the patriarchal values of the Nazi society. As noted earlier, the idea of the "Ideal Aryan" originated within the fascist National Socialist Movement propagating the manliness of *men in mass* to set themselves apart from the "inferior" Jewish people. Empowered within the Nazi culture, these perpetrators were stereotyped by the system as "bonding male camaraderie" and legally authorized to threaten and destroy the objectified body of the women. Mosse's statement—"The Nazis left nothing to chance, and the true German was meant to execute a set plan for the racial state, which was always supposed to grow organically out of the nation's past"— exemplifies the abuse inflicted on the female bodies and the degradation of the human being.[38] The female body is represented as the site of destruction and defined as an object to be eradicated at the moment of arrival. As the process of annihilation proceeds, the methodological unmaking of the human body is revealed in its naked condition. Lengyel remembers a scene in the face of nudity and certainty of death: "They were made to climb into a truck and were taken away, still entirely nude."[39] This sentence echoes Primo Levi's statement that the *Lager* was a factory for producing corpses before collectively being turned into ashes.[40]

Dr. Gisella Perl was prisoner No. 25404 in Auschwitz-Birkenau. In her memoir *I Was a Doctor in Auschwitz*, Perl writes, "I offer this book as a monument commemorating the events of the years 1940–1945, commemorating Nazi bestiality, Nazi sadism, Nazi inhumanity and the death of their six million innocent Jewish victims."[41] As this quote shows, Perl points out three categories that define the Nazi's systematic organization to "wipe out" the Jewish people from Europe. In chapters such as "Dr. Kapezius," "Arrival at Auschwitz (traveled 8 days)," "Roll Call," "Dinner at Auschwitz," "The Beauty Parlor," and "The Life-saving Embryo," Perl describes the evil acts of the Nazis. Known as the "Angel and Abortionist in the Auschwitz Death Camp," Perl was famous for saving the lives of hundreds of mothers by aborting their pregnancies, as pregnant mothers were often beaten and killed by Dr. Josef Mengele, the most infamous Nazi doctor.[42] On the treatment of pregnant women, she writes: "They were surrounded by a group of SS men and women, who amused themselves by giving these helpless creatures a taste of hell, after which death was a welcome friend. . . . They were beaten with clubs and whips, torn by dogs, dragged around by their hair and kicked in the stomach with heavy German boots. Then, when they collapsed, they were thrown into the crematory—alive."[43]

The witness testifies in her memoir to forced medical procedures and human care for the suffering women she treated in order to survive. She describes the physical conditions and the lack of sanitary or medical necessities. Reducing suffering and saving pregnant women had become Perl's reason to survive. To emphasize Perl's work as a female physician, Myrna Goldenberg gives a short biographical note describing the survivor as a woman who crossed national and private boundaries in order to become a physician.[44]

In contrast to Olga Lengyel who devotes the first chapter of her memoir to her family life in Eastern Europe, Gisela Perl draws attention to the systematic Nazi organization embodied within the personality of German scientist Dr. Kapezius. Perl begins her memoir with the chapter titled "Dr. Kapezius," describing the ever-increasing numbers of Nazi "conquerors" in Maramaros Sziget, Transylvania, in December 1943.[45] She writes, "To every Jewish mother, wife and sister, the German soldier was the symbol of all evil."[46] While working as a gynecologist in her office, she was approached by a "well-mannered German" with the name Dr. Kapezius. Denying his interest in the I. G. Farbenindustrie, the medical propagandist insisted upon a meeting with Dr. Perl and her husband to discuss Germany's past during the Weimar Republic and the possible return to pre-Hitler Germany after the Nazis were defeated. Perhaps most importantly, Perl testifies, "Five months later I was to see him again, in the second month of my stay in Auschwitz, clad in an SS *Hauptsturm-fuehrer* uniform. He was the Commander of the camp."[47] In seeing him as a Nazi perpetrator, it becomes clear for her that Dr. Kapezius's fake identity as an anti-Hitler citizen manipulated the couple's innocence to speak about their view on the Nazis only to have them deported to Auschwitz for annihilation. In the narrative, she describes how she fainted once she discovered the doctor's true identity.

When ordered by Dr. Mengele, the chief physician of the camp, to step out of line, she came face to face with Dr. Kapezius. In contrast to the seemingly common interest in the political situation and the rise of the Nazis, she narrates how she finds herself now in the position to face him as a Jewish female victim being exposed to his order from within the structure of the Nazi ideology. In mirroring the two specific situations, Perl's narrative testifies first to the manipulation of this German abusing the couple's humanity and innocence and second to using his position within the political power structure to have the family transported to Auschwitz.

How can one bear being forced to practice deadly methods in order to inflict cruel violence upon the Jewish women? What Perl describes of the Nazi-bestiality can be seen in the paradoxical yet systematic plan to brutally violate female bodies, in particular removing the fetuses from pregnant women. Being in the position of a Nazi perpetrator and knowing that Perl was a physician, he ordered her to work as a gynecologist without any instruments or medicine. "Jewish physicians step out of the lines!" Dr. Menerle, [Mengele], chief physician of the camp ordered. "We are going to establish a hospital. You are going to be the camp gynecologist."[48]

In the chapter on "Irma Greze," Perl remembers a life-threating situation in which Greze [Grese] asks her to perform an abortion on her even though it was strictly forbidden to touch a guard. Relieved that Irma Greze did not kill her, Perl writes: "I remembered all the pregnant women in the hospital . . . I remembered all the pregnant women in camp whose life depended on my skill, courage and readiness to help . . . and suddenly I knew why I had been spared. I was responsible for those women . . . I had to remain alive so as to save them from death . . . I was their doctor."[49]

In reading Perl's testimonies about the horrendous violations against the female bodies with the goal to undue a woman's most precious biological ability to bear children, it is important to remember Horowitz's claim that "women may remember differently from men—or they may remember different things."[50] Three episodes that speak of the unspeakable, making the reader speechless even seventy years after the liberation of Auschwitz on January 27, 1945, further illustrate Nazi bestiality, sadism, and inhumanity.[51]

SADISM

One of Dr. Josef Mengele's self-satisfying gratifications was inflicting pain upon the women's bodies, in particular the pregnant Jewish women. Perl remembers the perverse attitude of the SS physician combined with his evil desire for torture imposed upon the vulnerable and helpless female victims. She remembers: "We had no anesthetics, of course, and the screams of the unfortunate patients seemed to give Dr. Mengele a perverse pleasure." [52] In reading this quote, the reader can recall that the enclosed world of the concentration camp allowed the perpetrators to exercise absolute control, satisfying each individual malicious desire under the excuse of following orders.

In Lengyel's memoir, Perl also testifies to the denunciation of victims' bodies and the degrading order imposed upon the vulnerable women to entertain sadistic perpetrators, "One morning, at Zählappell (roll call), we had to lift our skirts and hold them up while laughing SS men walked through our lines whipping our naked bodies and selecting many among us to die in the lines as a punishment for having damaged camp property." [53] This episode makes clear that all privileges of being born human are lost and that the women were subjugated by the dominance of the oppressors. While the bestial SS males acknowledge their power over the Jewish women through acts of perverse laughter and brutal beating, the victims are captured in a struggle between life and death.

Within the larger context of women survivors of Nazi genocide, Horowitz notes that pregnancy in the camps turns into a life-threatening event not only for the mother and the baby but also for the community. She notes, "While many survivors chronicle or depict pregnancy (sometimes their own) in the ghettos and camps, pregnancy comes to mean different things in different accounts." [54] Central to Perl's eyewitness account is her chapter titled "The Life-Saving Embryo." [55] The Jewish physician remembers an order given by Dr. Mengele to abort a fetus:

> I shall always remember that day. I had been ordered to interrupt a two-month-old pregnancy and conserve the embryo in formalin.
> It was a difficult operation without instruments, without anesthetics, but Fate was merciful to me and I succeeded in bringing out the eight-week-old fetus in one piece. It was a beautiful specimen and I hurried to put it into the formalin jar to show it to Dr. Mengele later. [56]

The passage describes the obscene and crucial torture against the female body of an anonymous woman and her embryo. Instead of developing as a human being in the womb of its mother, the fetus was violently removed and preserved in its afterlife in a container of formalin. The brutality against the female body, in particular against Jewish women, is embodied in the figure of the jarred fetus. Perl's account suggests that for Dr. Mengele the conservation of the fetus symbolizes a token of Nazi power. Instead of a mother giving life to her child, the (possibly) eight-weeks old fetus is removed from the mother's womb not to save her life, but to terminate the pregnancy thus preventing another Jewish child being born into the world. In testifying to the surgical abortion procedure without instruments and without anesthetics, the impact on the psyche and the physical body of the maternal victim will not have vanished into ashes after the mother's death.

Dr. Perl's words express the unimaginable horror and pain of a life and death situation imposed by the lustful persecutor and mass murderer Dr. Mengele. The statement "I shall always remember that day," bears witness to the gravity of the inhuman order that seemed to be engraved forever in Perl's mind. The fact that a Jewish physician was found by Mengele to remove a fetus from the womb of a maternal body without instruments and without anesthetics points to the mental as well as the physical methods of "genocidal forces" of the systematic Nazi machine. Her words that the fetus "[It] was a beautiful specimen" evoke feelings of a belated justice that grants a special meaning to a developing unborn human life. As ordered, Perl puts the fetus into a container to conserve it for the monster Dr. Mengele and to also save her own life, "and I hurried to put it into the formalin jar to show it to Dr. Mengele later."

ETHICAL CHOICES

In reading the three specific passages, questions can be raised. How do we understand the two eyewitness accounts of Dr. Olga Lengyel and Dr. Gisella Perl written in the immediate aftermath of the Shoah? What do these writings reveal in terms of female survivors who experienced the Nazi crimes first hand? In his article "The Dilemma of Choice in the Deathcamps," Lawrence Langer defines his term "choiceless choice" as "critical decisions [that] did not reflect options between life and death, but between one form of 'abnormal' response and another, both imposed by a situation that was in no way of the victim's own choosing."[57] It is against the background of this quote, and also through the more specific categories of body and gender that the status of the female body is established in the discourse of Holocaust testimonies and Holocaust studies. But here the question remains: How can we understand the writing of the memoirs in terms of gender? Both female survivors construct a body of stories that attest to the loss of anonymous female bodies, and therefore simultaneously supplement these female bodies and inscribe their testimonies on these bodies.

In writing about the perpetration against women, Dr. Olga Lengyel and Dr. Gisella Perl's memoirs structure a new gendered narrative related to the female body. Their language is influenced by the asymmetrical relation between the women and their perpetrators. Not only do these writings constitute individual and collective identities, but they also assume a new gendered identity. In this sense, their stories uphold the constitution of the female writing/testimony. Dorota Glowacka argues Levinas's "ethics is a philosophy of peace and a cry against murder, which suspends ethics, on behalf of the Other to whom I am respon-sible."[58] It may be said that the two survivors not only reclaim the female bodies by giving testimony to the brutal events but also take part in the ethics of remembrance. Glowacka writes: "The decision to listen and re-spond to the Other's story, to assume its onus of pain and dread, is a difficult one."[59]

The memoirs written by survivors Olga Lengyel and Gisella Perl are narrative acts of reconstruction. They are acts of affirmation that give back life to all the women who had been forced to parade naked before the SS men, who have been publically displayed, who have had to abort their children to save their own lives even if for a short time, and to all the women who were tortured, degraded, and murdered under Hitler's ra-pacious ideology of promoting a master race. Having survived, these writers acknowledge their mortal life and embrace life after surviving death. It seems in writing each line, a new form of life can emerge. Their writings, even in telling of the murder of millions, are a rebuke to the Nazi attempt to make Europe "Judenrein." Despite the enormity of Nazi acts and the deaths they caused, they failed.

## NOTES

1. Olga Lengyel, *Five Chimneys: A Woman Survivor's True Story of Auschwitz* (Chica-go: Academy Chicago Publisher, 1995 [1947]).
2. Dr. Gisella Perl, *I was a Doctor in Auschwitz* (New York: Arno Press, 1979; 1948).
3. Sarah R. Horowitz, "Women in Holocaust Literature: Engendering Trauma Memory," in *Women in the Holocaust*, ed., Dalia Ofer and Lenore J. Weitzman (New Haven and London: Yale University Press, 1999), 366.
4. Sarah R. Horowitz, 366.
5. Judith Tydor Baumel, "Gender and Family Studies of the Holocaust: A Historio-graphical Overview," in *Lessons and Legacies: Teaching the Holocaust in a Changing World*, ed. Donald G. Schilling (Evanston: Northwestern University Press, 1998), 107–17.
6. Olga Lengyel, *Five Chimneys: A Woman Survivor's True Story of Auschwitz* (Chica-go: Academy Chicago Publisher, 1995 [1947]), 119.
7. *Five Chimneys*, 103.
8. Doris L. Bergen, "What do Studies of Women, Gender, and Sexuality Contribute to Understanding the Holocaust?," in Different *Horrors, Same Hell: Gender and the Holo-caust*, eds., Myrna Goldenberg and Amy H. Shapiro (Seattle: University of Washington Press, 2012), 17. Bergen notes that the first path-breaking studies on Women's Histo-ries of the Holocaust appeared in the 1980s followed by articles, monographs, and dissertations that appeared approximately three years later in a range of disciplines.
9. Joan Ringelheim, "Women and the Holocaust: A Reconsideration of Research," *Signs* 10, no. 4 (Summer 1985): 742.
10. Joan Ringelheim. "Women and the Holocaust. A Reconsideration of Research," in *Feminism and Community* ed. Penny A. Weiss and Marilyn Friedman (Philadelphia: Temple University Press, 1995), 318.
11. For a detailed list on gender and the Holocaust, see Doris L. Bergen, 30–37.
12. Cited from *Five Chimneys*. Cluj was called Klausenburg by German-speakers and Kolozsaur by Hungarians, 11.
13. Ibid., 11.

14. Ibid., 11–12.

15. Ibid., 13.

16. In March 1944, the Germans occupied Hungary and deported approximately 430,000 Hungarian Jews to Auschwitz. When the Holocaust ended more than 560,000 Hungarian Jews were dead. Most were murdered in the gas chambers at Auschwitz-Birkenau.

17. *Five Chimneys*, 18.

18. Ibid., 20.

19. Myrna Goldenberg and Amy H. Shapiro, *Different Horrors, Same Hell*, 3, 15.

20. John Berger, *Ways of Seeing: Based on the BBC Television Series* (London: British Broadcasting Corporation and Penguin Books, 1972), 54.

21. Ibid., 54.

22. Ibid., 52.

23. Emmanuel Levinas, *Existence & Existents*, trans. Alphonso Lingis, foreword, Robert Bernasconi (Pittsburgh: Duquesne University Press, 2001), 31.

24. Sybil Milton, "Sensitive Issues about Holocaust Films" in *Genocide: Critical Issues about the Holocaust. A Companion Volume to the Film Genocide*, eds., Alex Grobman, Daniel Landes, and Sybil Milton (Los Angeles: Simon Wiesenthal Center, 1983), 8.

25. *Five Chimneys*, 27.

26. Ibid., 25.

27. Ibid., 28.

28. Raoul Hilberg *The Destruction of European Jewry* (New York: Holmes & Meier, 1985).

29. George Lachman Mosse, "The New Fascist Man" in *The Image of Man: The Creation of Modern Masculinity* (New York: Oxford University Press, 1998), 156.

30. For more information on the Race Laws see: http://www.ushmm.org/learn/timeline-of-events/1933–1938/nuremberg-race-laws. *The new fascist man*, 169–70.

31. Mosse, 170.

32. Ibid., 170.

33. Ibid., 166.

34. Ibid., 176.

35. Ibid., 175.

36. Ibid., 150.

37. Ibid., 175.

38. Ibid., 164.

39. *Five Chimneys*, 51.

40. Levi, Primo, Survival in Auschwitz (New York: Macmillan Publishing Company, 1993).

41. *I Was a Doctor in Auschwitz*, 12.

42. Yisrael Gutman, Michael Berenbaum, ed., *Anatomy of the Auschwitz Death Camps* (Bloomington: Indiana University Press, 1994).

43. *I Was a Doctor in Auschwitz*, 80.

44. Myrna Goldenberg: Gisella Perl (1900–1988), in *An Encyclopedia of Writers and Their Work, Holocaust Literature: Lerner to Zychlinsky*, ed. S. Lillian Kremer (London: Routledge, 2003), 931–33.

45. *I was a Doctor in Auschwitz*, 13–20.

46. Ibid., 13.

47. Ibid., 16.

48. Ibid., 16.

49. Ibid., 65.

50. Sara R. Horowitz. "Women in the Holocaust," 366.

51. http://www.ushmm.org/information/exhibitions/online-features/special-focus/liberation-seventieth-anniversary.

52. *I was a Doctor in Auschwitz*, 76.

53. Ibid.

54. Sara R. Horowitz, "Women in Holocaust Literature," 268.

55. *I was a Doctor in Auschwitz*, 116–24.

56. Ibid., 116.

57. Lawrence Langer, "The Dilemma of Choice in the Deathcamps," in *Echoes from the Holocaust. Philosophical Reflections on a Dark Time*, ed. Alan Rosenberg and Gerald Eugene Myers (Philadelphia: Temple University Press, 1988), 120.

58. *Between Ethics and Aesthetics. Crossing the Boundaries*. Edited by Dorota Glowacka and Stephen Boss (Albany: State University of New York Press, 2002), 100.

59. Ibid., 104.

# Epilogue

*Gendered Testimonies of the Holocaust: Writing Life*, examines the works of Paul Celan (1920–1970), Charlotte Delbo (1913–1985), Olga Lengyel (1908–2001), Gisella Perl (1907–1988), and Dan Pagis (1930–1986). At the time of writing poetry and prose to testify to the atrocious crimes of the Nazi camp system, each individual experienced immeasurable suffering, extreme betrayal, unspeakable loss, and unimaginable physical and psychological violence. Incarcerated in various Nazi forced labor camps and Auschwitz, Celan, Delbo, Lengyel, Pagis, and Perl survived even though by all expectations they should have died. Each work attests to survivor-writers profound yearning to tell stories of life and death to ensure that the memory of those who died an innocent death would not be forgotten.

Confronted with different forms of testimony, I found myself in the position of a reader struggling with the fact that I am originally from Germany, and that I was facing the stories of people who were arbitrarily and with sadistic enjoyment tortured by Hitler's regime to "purify" Germany of European Jewry. However, the works of these survivors had such a profound impact on my first and continued readings that I revisited them for this monograph.

*Gendered Testimonies of the Holocaust: Writing Life* examines the relation between the subject and other, and the text and it's other. I have taken a special interest in the gendered aspect of these pairings and relations they presume. My book's overarching premise—that writing as survival is ineradicably an affirmation of life—involves an interpretive take on a long tradition of studies on testimony and language in the context of the Holocaust. Each reading reflects the work of so many dedicated and eminent scholars who have explored the poetry and prose of the survivors at the same time producing literary, historical, and theoretical responses. Based on the vast amount of scholarship within the last sixty years, I have engaged with the works of thinkers to explore new ideas. In addition, the ability to visit the United States Holocaust Memorial Museum and to research from the vast amount of historical resources has been indispensable to me.

Given the shared ground in relation to the themes of life and death after surviving the Shoah, the work of Jacques Derrida, Emmanuel Levinas, and Jean-François Lyotard were indispensable for the framework of my book. In Jacques Derrida's last interview given to *Le Monde* shortly before his death, the French Jewish philosopher addresses the themes of life and death. In taking his own mortality into account, he admitted to experiencing life as a repeated survival. As discussed, Derrida conceptualized survival as the opposition between life and death brings together the oddly paired connotations of "an unconditional affirmation of life" and "living the most intense life possible." Influenced by Walter Benjamin, Derrida explains the German Jewish cultural critic's terms of *"überleben"* (which is to live after death) and *"fortleben"* (which is to continue to live). Based on Derrida's philosophical thinking that emerges out of his personal experience, I focused on the opposition between life and death and the claim that each survivor's testimony attests to an unconditional affirmation of life after survival undeniably linked to the act of writing. Furthermore, the attempt to give testimony symbolizes writing as the act of giving birth to restructure the survivor's identity. Influenced by the work of the Jewish survivor and French philosopher Emmanuel Levinas, especially his concept of the ethical subject, I suggest, ensures the survivor's most intense life possible. By providing a memorial space in which the ones who are dead can live on, the ethical response to the other equally marks the survivor's survival as the most intense life possible. In addition, I enter the conversation on maternity as the ultimate ethical response to address the writing of male and female writers. Levinas's metaphorical thinking of motherhood is embedded within the Jewish tradition. Although the notion of feminism has been critically viewed by prominent feminists/philosophers/thinkers such as Luce Irigaray, Stella Sanford, Julia Kristeva Monique Schneider, Tina Chanter, Catherine Chalier or John Llewelyn and explored in Claire Katz's essay "From Eros to Maternity: Love, Death, and 'the Feminine' in the Philosophy of Emmanuel Levinas," Levinas's notion of "maternity" brings together the female and male survivors who exemplify the relationship between the ethical subject and the Other. In these examples two males wrote poetry and the three women have written narratives. We cannot draw any conclusions from such a small sample nor suggest that one form is more likely to occur with men or with women. Nelly Sachs wrote powerful poetry that grew out of the Holocaust. Each author gravitated to a form that served best.

The four chapters of this book are framed in light of these two philosophical thinkers. It was my attempt to provide a strong theoretical background for the first three chapters. The use of the interdisciplinary theoretical scholarship merits my sincere thanks. Without such creative innovations the continuation of academic discourse would not be possible. The fourth chapter describes the violence imposed upon the female victims. Lengyel and Perl were forced to labor in the Nazi's so-called hospital, under the supervision of Dr. Josef Mengele. The women always knew they were just one step from being murdered in the gas chambers should they not follow any order. I wanted to draw attention to the torture, treatment, and murder of pregnant Jewish women and their children. The discomfort that comes from reading such testimonies and remembering what one group of humans did to another group cannot be avoided.

In the first chapter, "A Mother's Testimony as a Dwelling Place," Dan Pagis writes from the perspective of a female victim who pencils a text on the walls of a railroad car. Pagis creates the figure of a mother as the symbol of life and love who addresses an unknown reader to give her son a message that she cannot bring herself to articulate before she dies. We as the reader are left with the responsibility for the other and at the same time are charged with preventing such crimes against humanity.

In the second chapter, "Remembrance of the M/other/tongue," Celan writes from the position of the mute poet calling out for his mother within himself. The poem attests to the fact that the remembrance of the mother sparks the return to his mother tongue again. In calling his absent mother for help to create a poem, Celan communicates the crisis he faces in writing in German, the language used by the Nazis. It becomes clear that the poet can only begin writing again in the German language by remembering the mother.

In the third chapter, "The Maternal Function of Giving Testimony," the narrator describes an event experienced by group of female prisoners in the concentration camp. The unexpected appearance of Alice's wooden leg pulls memories from the depths to the surface of a traumatic experience in which the women were forced to leave their friend alone who was dying in front of their eyes. The unexpected return of an anonymous wooden leg exemplifies the impact of trauma. The chapter not only describes the conflict between knowing and not knowing but also the writing of the event. The story shows the artificial leg has a prosthetic function for writing the text. The story shows how writing embodies a maternal function, and how Delbo creates a vibrant remembrance amidst death.

In the fourth chapter, "Embodied Existence of Mothers," the Eastern European Jewish women, Olga Lengeyl and Gisella Perl, testify to the most sadistic violation of the female bodies and the enjoyment of Nazi perpetrators in the camps to dehumanize the women. The reader learns through Perl's memoir new arrivals were publically exposed and how the guards transformed the space of human suffering into a spectacle for drunken and violent men. Lengyel testifies to the experimental methods of Dr. Mengele that defy human imagination and yet became a reality for an uncountable number of pregnant women. We learn about the doctors' forcing women to choose between life and death. The memoirs of the women embody the existence of mothers so that they can be remembered and continue to live as mothers who once upon a time brought life into the world.

*Gendered Testimonies of the Holocaust: Writing Life* frames in particular the philosophical concepts of Jacques Derrida and Emmanuel Levinas. Starting from the premise that survival is ineradicably an affirmation of life, I show how the figure of maternity as the ultimate ethical response in relation to the other makes the most intense life possible.

# Select Bibliography

The study of this topic required reading over a wide body of literature that either touched the topic directly or explored aspects on the periphery. This bibliography reflects that reading rather than only the works I have cited in the body of the text and upon which my thesis was founded. It should serve the reader who wishes to make a more wide-ranging tour through the narratives that have been produced as people attempt to understand the victims, the survivors, and the perpetrators.

Adorno, Theodor. *Aesthetic Theory*. Translated by C. Lenhardt. New York: Routledge, 1986.
———. "Commitment." In *Notes to Literature II*. Edited by Rolf Tiedemann. Translated by Shierry Weber Nicholson. New York: Columbia University Press, 1992.
Agamben, Giorgio. *Remnants of Auschwitz: The Witness and the Archive*. Translated by Daniel Heller-Roazen. New York: Zone Books, 1999.
Alphen, E. Van. *Caught by History*. Stanford: Stanford University Press, 1977.
Antelme, Robert. *L'espèce humaine*. Paris: Gallimard, 1957.
Arendt, Hannah. *Eichmann in Jerusalem: A Report on the Banality of Evil*. Revised Edition. New York: Penguin, 1965.
———. "The Concentration Camps." In *A Holocaust Reader: Responses to the Nazi Extermination*. Edited by Michael L. Morgan. New York and Oxford: Oxford University Press, 2001.
Baer, Ulrich. *Remnants of Song: Trauma and the Experience of Modernity in Charles Baudelaire and Paul Celan*. Stanford: Stanford University Press, 2000.
———. *Spectacle Evidence: The Photography of Trauma*. Cambridge, MA and London: MIT Press, 2002.
Ball, Karyn. *Disciplining the Holocaust*. Albany: State University of New York Press, 2008.
Bataille, George. *Story Of The Eye: By Lord Auch*. Translated by Joachim Neugroschal. New York: Urizen Book, 1977.
Bender, John and David E. Wellbery, eds. *The Ends of Rhetoric. History, Theory, Practice*. Stanford: Stanford University Press, 1990.
Bennington, Geoffrey. *Lyotard: Writing the Event*. Manchester: Manchester University Press, 1987.
Benveniste, Émile. *Problèmes de linguistique générale*. Paris: Gallimard, 1966–1974.
Bergen, Doris L. *War & Genocide. A Concise History of the Holocaust*. 2nd ed. Lanham, MD: Rowman & Littlefield Publishers, Inc., 2009.
Blanchot, Maurice. *L'entretien infini*. Paris: Gallimard, 1969.
———. *L'écriture du désastre*. Paris: Gallimard, 1980.
———. *Le Dernier à parler*. Montpellier: Fata Morgana, 1984.
———. *The Writing of the Disaster*. Translated by Ann Smock. Lincoln: University of Nebraska Press, 1986.
Buck, Theo: *Muttersprache. Mördersprache*. Celan-Studien I. Aachen: Rimbaud, 1993.
———. *L'instant de ma mort*. Saint Clément-la-Rivière: Fata Morgana, 1994.

————. *The Instant of My Death/Maurice Blanchot. Demeure: Fiction and Testimony/Jacques Derrida*. Translated by Elizabeth Rottenberg. Stanford: Stanford University Press, 2000.

Bollack, Jean. "Paul Celan über die Sprache: Das Gedicht 'Sprachgitter' und seine Interpretationen." *Paul Celan*. Herausgegeben von Werner Hamacher und Winfried Menninghaus. Suhrkamp Taschenbuch Materialien. Frankfurt: Suhrkamp Verlag, 1988.

Bracher, Nathan. "Histoire, ironie et interprétation chez Charlotte Delbo: Une écriture d'Auschwitz," *French Forum* 19, no.1 (1994): 81–93.

*Brockhaus Enzyklopädie in vierundzwanzig Bänden: Sechster Band DS–EW und erster Nachtrag*. Mannheim: F. A. Brockhaus, 1998.

Bron, Anthony J., Ramesh C. Tripathi, and Brenda J. Tripathi. *Wolff's Anatomy of the Eye and Orbit*, 8th ed. London: Chapman & Hall, 1997.

Browning, Christopher R. *Ordinary Men: Reserve Battalion 101 and the Final Solution in Poland*. New York: Harper Collins, 1992.

Bruns, Gerald L. "Blanchot/Celan: Désœuvrement." In *Maurice Blanchot: The Refusal of Philosophy*. Baltimore and London: Johns Hopkins University Press, 1997.

————. "Blanchot/Celan: Unterwegssein." In *Maurice Blanchot: The Refusal of Philosophy*. Baltimore and London: The Johns Hopkins University Press, 1997.

Buber, Martin. "The Dialogue between Heaven and Earth." In *Holocaust Reader: Responses to the Nazi Extermination*, ed. Michael L. Morgan, 63–77. New York and Oxford: Oxford University Press, 2001.

Cadava, Eduardo. *Words Of Light: Theses on The Photography of History*. Princeton, NJ: Princeton University Press, 1997.

Caro, Del Adrian. *The Early Poetry of Paul Celan: In the Beginning Was the Word*. Baton Rouge and London: Louisiana State University Press, 1997.

Caruth, Cathy. "An Interview with Robert Jay Lifton." In *Trauma: Explorations in Memory*, ed. Cathy Caruth, 128–147. Baltimore and London: Johns Hopkins University Press, 1995.

————. *Literature in the Ashes of History*. Baltimore: Johns Hopkins University Press, 2013.

————. "Parting Words: Trauma, Silence and Survival." In *Between Psyche and Polis: Refiguring History in Literature and Theory*, ed. Michael Rossington and Anne Whitehead, 77–96. Aldershot: Ashgate, 2000.

————, ed. *Trauma. Explorations in Memory*. With introductions by Cathy Caruth. Baltimore and London: Johns Hopkins University Press, 1995.

————. *Unclaimed Experience: Trauma, Narrative, and History*. Baltimore: Johns Hopkins University Press, 1996.

Celan, Paul. "Der Meridian: Speech on the occasion of the receiving of the Georg Büchner Prize, Darmstadt, October 22, 1960." In *Paul Celan: Collected Prose*. Translated by Rosemarie Waldrop. Manchester: Carcanet Press, 1986.

————. "Speech on the Occasion of Receiving the Literature Prize of the Free Hanseatic City of Bremen." In *Paul Celan: Collected Prose*. Translated by Rosemarie Waldrop. Manchester: Carcanet Press, 1986.

————. "Ansprache anlässlich der Entgegennahme des Literaturpreises der Freien Hansestadt Bremen." In Dritter Band, *Gesammelte Werke in sieben Bänden*. Suhrkamp Taschenbuch 3204. Frankfurt: Suhrkamp Taschenbuch Verlag, 2000.

————. "Der Meridian: Rede anläßlich der Verleihung des Georg-Büchner-Preises Darmstadt, am 22 Oktober 1960." In Dritter Band, *Gesammelte Werke in sieben Bänden*. Suhrkamp Taschenbuch 3402. Frankfurt: Suhrkamp Taschenbuch Verlag, 2000.

————. "Sprachgitter." In Erster Band, *Gesammelte Werke in sieben Bänden*. Suhrkamp Taschenbuch 3202. Frankfurt: Suhrkamp Taschenbuch Verlag, 2000.

————. "Sprich auch Du." In Erster Band, *Gesammelte Werke in sieben Bänden*. Suhrkamp Taschenbuch 3202. Frankfurt: Suhrkamp Taschenbuch Verlag, 2000.

———. "Speak You Too." In *Selected Poems and Prose of Paul Celan*. Translated by John Felstiner. New York and London: W. W. Norton, 2001.

———. "Speech-Grille." In *Selected Poems and Prose of Paul Celan*. Translated by John Felstiner. New York and London: W. W. Norton, 2001.

Chare, Nicholas. *Auschwitz and Afterimages: Abjections, Witnessing and Representation*. London: I. B. Tauris Press, 2011.

Clementi, Federica K. *Holocaust Mothers & Daughters. Family, History and Trauma*. Waltham, MA: Brandeis University Press.

Clendinnen, Inga. *Reading The Holocaust*. Cambridge: Cambridge University Press, 1999.

Colin, Amy. *Paul Celan: Hologram of Darkness*. Bloomington and Indianapolis: Indiana University Press. 1991.

Delbo, Charlotte. *Les belles lettres*. Paris: Minuit, 1961.

———. *Le convoi du 24 Janvier*. Paris: Minuit, 1965.

———. "La jambe d'Alice." In *Aucun de nous ne reviendra*. Paris: Minuit, 1970.

———. "Le Même Jour." In *Aucun de nous ne reviendra*. Paris: Minuit, 1970.

———. "Mado." *Mesure de nos jours*. Paris: Minuit, 1971.

———. *Une conaissance inutile*. Paris: Minuit, 1971.

———. *Qui rapportera ces paroles?* Paris: P. J. Oswald, 1974.

———. *Spectres, mes compagnons*. Lausanne: Maurice Bridel, 1977.

———. "Who Will Carry the Word?" In *The Theatre of the Holocaust*, ed. Robert Skloot. Translated by Cynthia Haft. Madison: The University of Wisconsin Press, 1982.

———. *La mémoire et les jours*. Paris: Berg International, 1985.

———. *Days and Memory*. Translated by Rosette Lamont. Marlboro, VT: Marlboro Press, 1990.

———. "Alice's Leg." In *Auschwitz and After*. With an introduction by Lawrence L. Langer. Translated by Rosette C. Lamont. New Haven and London: Yale University Press, 1995.

———. "Mado." In *Auschwitz and After*. With an introduction by Lawrence L. Langer. Translated by Rosette C. Lamont. New Haven and London: Yale University Press, 1995.

———. "The Same Day." In *Auschwitz and After*. With an introduction by Lawrence L. Langer. Translated by Rosette C. Lamont. New Haven and London: Yale University Press, 1995.

———. *Convoy to Auschwitz: Women of the French Resistance*. Translated by Carol Cosman. Boston: Northeastern University Press, 1997.

Derrida, Jacques. *Cinders*. Translated, edited, and with an introduction by Ned Lukacher. Lincoln: University of Nebraska Press, 1991.

———. *Demeure: Maurice Blanchot*. Paris: Galilée, 1998.

———. *Learning to Live Finally: The Last Interview*. Introduction by Jean Birnbaum. Translated by Pascale-Anne Brault and Michael Naas. New York: Melville House Publishing, 2007. Originally published in French as *Apprendre à vivre enfin. Entretien avec Jean Birnbaum*. Paris: Éditions Galilée, 2005. The interview with Jean Birnbaum appeared in *Le Monde* 19 August 2004.

———. "Living On: Border Lines." In *Deconstruction and Criticism*, ed. Harold Bloom et al., 75–176. New York: Seabury, 1979.

———. *Memoirs of the Blind: The Self-Portrait and Other Ruins*. Translated by Pascale-Anne Brault and Michael Naas. Chicago: University of Chicago Press, 1993.

———. *Monolingualism of the Other; or, The Prosthesis of Origin*. Translated by Patrick Mensah. Cultural Memory in the Present. Mieke Bal and Hent de Vries, Editors. Stanford, CA: Stanford University Press, 1998.

———. *Points . . . Interviews, 1974–1993*. Edited by Elisabeth Weber. Translated by Peggy Kamuf and others. Stanford: Stanford University Press: 1995, 143 (Originally published in French as *Points de suspension. Entretiens by* Éditions Galilée, 1992.

———. *Schibboleth pour Paul Celan*. Collection La philosophie en effect. Paris: Éditions Galilée, 1986.

———. "Ulysses Gramophone: Hear say yes in Joyce." Translated by François Raffoul. In *Acts of Literature*. Edited by Derek Attridge. New York: Routledge, 1992.

———. "White Mythology." In *Margins of Philosophy*, trans. Alan Bass, 207–71. Chicago: University of Chicago Press, 1982.

———. *The Work of Mourning*, ed. Pascale-Anne Brault and Michael Nass. Chicago and London: The University of Chicago Press, 2001.

Descartes, René. *Discourse on Method and the Meditations*. Translated by F. E. Sutcliffe. Harmondsworth: Penguin, 1979.

*Dtv-Lexikon in 20 Bänden: Band 6, Fli-Gev*. München: Deutscher Taschenbuch Verlag, 1997.

Dutoit, Thomas and Outi Pasanen. *Sovereignties in Question*. New York: Fordham University Press, 2005.

Elbert, Jerome W. "The Ancient Origins of the Idea of the Soul." In *Are Souls Real?* Amherst, NY: Prometheus Books, 2000.

Epstein, Julia and Lefkovitz Lori Hope, eds. *Shaping Losses: Cultural Memory and the Holocaust*. Urbana and Chicago: University of Illinois Press, 2001.

Eshel, Amir. "Von Kafka bis Celan: Deutsch-Jüdische Schriftsteller und ihr Verhältnis zum Hebräischen und Jiddischen." In Brenner, ed., *Jüdische Sprachen*, 96–108.

———. *Zeit der Zäsur: Jüdische Dichter im Angesicht der Shoah*. Band 169, Beiträge zur Neueren Literaturgeschichte. Heidelberg: Universitätsverlag C. Winter, 1999.

Ezrahi DeKoven, Sidra. *Booking Passage: Exile and Homecoming in the Modern Jewish Imagination*. Berkeley and Los Angeles: University of California Press, 2000.

———. *By Words Alone: The Holocaust in Literature*. With a foreword by Alfred Kazin. Chicago and London: University of Chicago Press, 1980.

———. "Representing Auschwitz." *History and Memory* 7, no. 2 (1966): 121–54.

Feinstein, Stephen C. *Absence/Presence: Critical Essays on the Artistic Memory of the Holocaust*. Syracuse: Syracuse University Press, 2005.

Felman, Shoshana and Dori Laub. M.D. *Testimony: Crises of Witnessing in Literature, Psychoanalysis, and History*. New York: Routledge, 1992.

———. *The Juridical Unconscious: Trials and Traumas In The Twentieth Century*. Cambridge, MA and London: Harvard University Press, 2002: 131–166.

Felstiner, John. *Paul Celan: Poet, Survivor, Jew*. New Haven and London: Yale University Press, 1995.

———. *Selected Poems and Prose of Paul Celan*. Translated by John Felstiner. New York and London: W. W. Norton, 2001.

Fioretes, Aris. *The Gray Book*. Stanford: Stanford University Press, 1994.

———, ed. *Word Traces: Reading of Paul Celan*. Baltimore and London: Johns Hopkins University Press, 1994.

Foley, Barbara. "Fact, Fiction, Fascism: Testimony and Mimesis in Holocaust Narratives." *Comparative Literature* 34, no. 4 (1982): 330–60.

Fóti, Véronique M. "The Dimension of Color." *International Studies in Philosophy* 22, no. 3: 13–28.

Freud, Sigmund. "Mourning and Melancholia." In Vol. 14, *The Standard Edition of the Complete Psychological Works*. Translated by J. Strachey, 243–58. London: Hogarth, 1953–1974.

———. *Beyond the Pleasure Principle*. With an introduction by Gregory Zilboorg. With a biographical introduction by Peter Gay. Translated and edited by James Strachey. New York and London: W. W. Norton and Company, 1961.

———. *The Interpretation of Dreams*. With an introduction and notes by Ritchie Robertson. Translated by Jocye Crick. Oxford and New York: Oxford University Press, 1999.

Friedlander, Henry. *The Origins of Nazi-Genocide: From Euthanasia to the Final Solution*. Chapel Hill: University of North Carolina Press, 1995.

Friedlander, Saul. *Memory, History, and the Extermination of the Jews of Europe*. Bloomington: Indiana University Press, 1993.

Fynsk, Christopher. "The Realities at Stake in a Poem: Celan's Bremen and Darmstadt Adresses." In *Word Traces: Readings of Paul Celan*. Edited by Aris Fioretes. Baltimore and London: The Johns Hopkins University Press, 1994.

Gigliotti, Simone. *The Train Journey: Transit, Captivity, and Witnessing the Holocaust*. New York: Berghahn, 2009.

Glenn, Jerry. "Celan's Transformation of Benn's 'Südwort.'" *German Life and Letters* 21 (1967): 12–13.

———. *Paul Celan*. New York: Twayne Publishers, 1973.

Glowacka, Dorota. *Disappearing Traces. Holocaust Testimonials, Ethics, and Aesthetics*. Seattle and London: University of Washington Press, 2012.

Goldenberg, Myrna and Amy H. Shapiro, eds. *Different Horrors, Same Hell. Gender and The Holocaust*. Seattle and London: University of Washington Press, 2013.

Gubar, Susan. *Poetry After Auschwitz. Remembering What One Never Knew*. Bloomington and Indianapolis: Indiana University Press, 2003.

Haft, Cynthia. *The Theme of Nazi Concentration Camps in French Literature*. The Hague and Paris: Mouton, 1973.

Hamacher, Werner. "Die Sekunde der Inversion: Bewegungen einer Figur durch Celans Gedichte." In *Paul Celan*. Herausgegeben von Werner Hamacher und Winfried Menninghaus. Suhrkamp Materialien. Suhrkamp Taschenbuch 2083. Frankfurt: Suhrkamp Verlag, 1988.

———, and Winfried Menninghaus, Herausgeber. *Paul Celan*. Suhrkamp Materialien. Suhrkamp Taschenbuch 2083. Frankfurt: Suhrkamp Verlag, 1988.

Hartman, Geoffrey H. *Saving The Text: Literature/Derrida/Philosophy*. Baltimore and London: Johns Hopkins University Press, 1981.

———. "Introduction: Darkness Visible." *Holocaust Remembrance: The Shapes of Memory*, ed. Geoffrey H. Hartman, 1–22. Cambridge, MA and Oxford: Blackwell, 1995.

———. *The Longest Shadow: In the Aftermath of the Holocaust*. Bloomington: Indiana University Press, 1996.

Hatley, James. *Suffering Witness. The Quandary of Responsibility after the Irreparable*. SUNY Series in Aesthetics and Philosophy of Art. New York: State University of New York Press, 2000.

Heidegger, Martin. *Unterwegs zur Sprache*. vol. 12, *Gesamtausgabe*. Frankfurt: Klostermann, 1985.

Heilmann, Markus. "Recalling the Event of 'a Word': Paul Celan's Volume 'Sprachgitter.'" *The Poetics of Memory*, ed. Thomas Wägenbaur, 135–143. Tübingen: Stauffenburg Verlag, 1998.

Heyne, M., Br. Crome, H. Meyer, and S. Seedorf, Hrsg. *Deutsches Wörterbuch von Jacob und Wilhelm Grimm*. Deutscher Taschenbuch Verlag: München, 1984.

Hilberg, Raul. *The Destruction of European Jewry*. New York and London: Holmes & Meier, 1985.

Hirsch, Marianne. "Family Pictures: Maus and Post-Memory." *Discourse* 15, no. 2 (1992–93): 3–29.

———. *Family Frames: Photography, Narrative, and Postmemory*. Cambridge, MA: Harvard University, 1997.

———. "The Generation of Postmemory." *Poetics Today* 29.1 (2008): 103–28.

Hornstein, Shelley, ed. *Impossible Images. Contemporary Art After the Holocaust*. New York: University Press, 2003.

Horowitz, Sara. *Voicing the Void: Muteness and Memory in Holocaust Fiction*. Albany: State University of New York Press, 1997.

Huyssen, Andreas. *Twilight Memories: Marking Time in a Culture of Amnesia*. New York: Routledge, 1995.

Janz, Marlies. *Vom Engagement absoluter Poesie. Zur Lyrik und Aesthetik Paul Celans*. Frankfurt: Autoren-und Verlagsgesellschaft Syndikat, 1976.

Johnson, Barbara. *Mother Tongues: Sexuality, Trials, Motherhood, Translation*. Cambridge, MA: Harvard University Press, 2003.

Kaplan, Ann. *Trauma Culture: The Politics of Terror and Loss in Media and Literature.* New Brunswick: Rutgers University Press, 2005.

Kaplan, Brett Ashley. "Pleasure, Memory, and Time Suspension in Holocaust Literature: Celan and Delbo." *Comparative Literature Studies* 38.4 (2001): 310–329.

———. *Unwanted Beauty: Aesthetic Pleasure in Holocaust Representation.* Chicago: University of Illinois Press, 2007.

Katz, Elise Claire. "From Eros to Maternity: Love, Death and "the Feminine" in *The Philosophy of Emmanuel Levinas.* Edited by Hava Tirosh-Samuelson. Bloomington: Indiana University Press, 2004.

Kelletat, Alfred. "Accessus zu Celans 'Sprachgitter.'" *Über Paul Celan,* Hrsg. Meinecke, Dietlind. Frankfurt: Suhrkamp Verlag, 1973: 113–137.

———. *Unwanted Beauty. Aesthetic Pleasure in Holocaust Representation.* Urbana and Chicago: University of Illinois Press, 2007.

Kiedaisch, Petra. *Lyrik nach Auschwitz? Adorno und die Dichter.* Stuttgart: Philipp Reclam, 1995.

Kincaid, Renée A. "Charlotte Delbo's 'Auschwitz et après': The Struggle for Signification." *French Forum* 9, no. 1 (1984): 98–109.

Kofman, Sarah. *Smothered Words.* Translated by Madeleine Dobie. Evanston: Northwestern University Press, 1998.

Kremer, Lilian S. *Women's Holocaust Writing: Memory and Imagination.* Lincoln and London: University of Nebraska Press, 1999.

LaCapra, Dominick. *History and Memory after Auschwitz.* Ithaca, NY: Cornell University Press, 1998.

Lacoue-Labarthe, Philippe. *La poésie comme experience.* Paris: Christian Bourgois Éditeur, 1986.

Lamont, Rosette C. "Literature, the Exile's Agent of Survival: Alexander Solzhenitsyn and Charlotte Delbo." *Mosaic* 9, no. 1 (1975): 1–17.

———. "Charlotte Delbo's Frozen Friezes." *L'Esprit Créateur* 2 (Summer 1979): 65–74.

Lang, Berel, ed. *Writing and the Holocaust.* New York and London: Holmes and Meier, 1988.

Langer Lawrence L. *The Age of Atrocity: Death in Modern Literature.* Boston: Beacon Press, 1978.

———. *Admitting the Holocaust.* New York: Oxford University Press, 1995.

———. *Holocaust Testimonies: The Ruins of Memory.* New Haven: Yale University Press, 1995.

Lanzmann, Claude. *Shoah.* Paris: Gallimard, 1985.

———. *Au sujet de Shoah: Le film de Claude Lanzmann.* Paris: Editions Belin, 1990.

———. "The Obscenity of Understanding: An Evening with Claude Lanzmann." *Trauma: Explorations in Memory,* ed. Cathy Caruth, 200–220. Baltimore and London: Johns Hopkins University Press, 1995.

Laplanche, Jean. *Life and Death in Psychoanalysis.* Translated with an introduction by Jeffrey Mehlman. Baltimore and London: Johns Hopkins University Press, 1976.

Laub, Dori, M.D. "An Event Without a Witness: Truth, Testimony and Survival." *Testimony: Crisis of Witnessing in Literature, Psychoanalysis, and History,* ed. Shoshana Felman and Dori Laub, M.D., 75–92. New York and London: Routledge, 1992.

Levi, Primo. *Survival in Auschwitz.* Translated by Stuart Woolf. New York: Collier, 1961.

———. *The Drowned and the Saved.* Translated by Raymond Rosenthal. New York: Vintage, 1989.

Levinas, Emmanuel. *Otherwise than Being, or Beyond Essence.* Translated by Alphonso Lingis. Pittsburgh: Duquesne University Press, 1998.

———. "Paul Celan: De l'être à l'autre." In *Noms propres.* Paris: Fata Morgana, 1976.

———. *Totality and Infinity: An Essay on Exteriority.* Translated by Alphonso Lingis. Pittsburgh: Duquesne University Press, 1998.

———. "Useless Suffering." In *Entre Nous: Thinking-of-the-Other.* New York: Columbia University, 1998.

Levine, Michael G. *The Belated Witness. Literature, Testimony, and the Question of Holocaust Survival*. Stanford: Stanford University Press, 2006.

Lipstadt, Deborah. *Denying the Holocaust*. New York: Free Press, 1993.

Liss, Andrea. *Trespassing through Shadows: Memory, Photography, and the Holocaust*. Minneapolis: University of Minnesota Press, 1998.

Lyon, James. "'Ganz und gar nicht hermetisch': Überlegungen zum 'richtigen' Lesen von Paul Celan's Lyrik." In *Psalm und Hawdalah: Zum Werk Paul Celans*, ed. Joseph Strelka, 171–91. Bern: Peter Lang, 1987.

Lyotard, Jean-François. *The Differend: Phrases in Dispute*. Translated by Georges Van de Abbeele. Minneapolis: University of Minnesota Press, 1988.

———. *Heidegger and "The Jews."* Translated by Andreas Michel and Mark Roberts. Minneapolis: University of Minnesota Press, 1990.

———. *The Inhuman: Reflections on Time*. Translated by Geoffrey Bennington and Rachel Bowlby. Stanford: Stanford University Press, 1991.

———. "The Survivor." In *Towards the Postmodern*. Edited by Robert Harvey and Mark S. Roberts. Amherst: New York: Humanities Press, 1995. (Originally published in French as *La Condition postmoderne: Rapport sur le savoir*. Les Éditions de Minuit. 1979).

Man, Paul de. *Blindness and Insight: Essays in the Rhetoric of Contemporary Criticism*, 2nd ed., revised. With an introduction by Wlad Godzich. vol. 7, Theory and History of Literature. Minneapolis: University of Minnesota Press, 1983.

———. *Aesthetic Ideology*. With an introduction and translated by Andrzey Warminski. Vol. 65, Theory and History of Literature. Minneapolis and London: University of Minnesota Press, 1996.

Marder, Elissa. *The Mother in the Age of Mechanical Reproduction. Psychoanalysis, Photography, Deconstruction*. New York: Fordham University Press, 2012.

McGlothlin, Erin Heather. *Second Generation Holocaust Literature: Legacies of Survival and Perpetration*. Rochester: Camden House, 2006.

Meinecke, Dietlind. *Wort Und Name Bei Paul Celan. Zur Widerruflichkeit des Gedichts*. Bd. 2, Literatur und Reflexion, hrsg. Beda Allemann. Bad Homburg, Berlin, Zürich: Verlag Gehlen. 1970.

———, hrsg. *Über Paul Celan*. Frankfurt: Suhrkamp Verlag, 1973.

Mendles-Flohr, Paul. *German Jews: A Dual Identity*. New Haven and London: Yale University Press, 1999.

Merleau-Ponty, Maurice. *The Visible and The Invisible*. Evanston: Northwestern University Press, 1968.

Miller, Nancy K. and Jason Tougaw, eds. *Trauma, Testimony and Community*. Urbana and Chicago: University of Illinois Press, 2002.

Nader, Andrés J. "The Shock of Arrival: Poetry from the Nazi Camps at the End of the Century." *Poetics Today* 21, no. 1 (2000): 151–86.

Newmark, Kevin. "Traumatic Poetry: Charles Baudelaire and the Shock of Laughter." In *Trauma: Explorations in Memory*. Edited by Cathy Caruth. Baltimore and London: Johns Hopkins University Press, 1995.

Nora, Pierre. "Between Memory and History: Les Lieux de Mémoire." *Representations* 26 (Spring 1989): 7–25.

Ofer, Dalia and Leonore J. Weitzman, eds. *Women in the Holocaust*. New Haven and London: Yale University Press, 1998.

Pajević, Marko. *Zur Poetik Paul Celans: Gedicht und Mensch — die Arbeit am Sinn*. Bd. 177, Beiträge zur Neueren Literaturgeschichte. Heidelberg: Universitätsverlag Winter, 2000.

Patterson, David. *Hebrew Language and Jewish Thought*. London and New York: Routledge Curzon, 2005.

Plass, Ulrich. "Language and History" in Theodor W. Adorno's *Notes to Literature*. New York: Routledge, 2007.

Poppenhusen, Astrid. *Durchkreuzung der Tropen: Paul Celans Die Niemandrose im Lichte der traditionellen Metaphorologie und ihrer Dekonstruktion*. Bd. 184, Beiträge zur Neueren Literaturgeschichte. Heidelberg: Universitätsverlag Winter, 2001.

Perl, Gisela. *I Was a Doctor in Auschwitz*. Salem, NH: Ayer Company, 1984.

———. *I Was a Doctor in Auschwitz*. Authorized facsimile of the original book, printed by microfilm-xerography on acid-free paper. Ann Arbor: University Microfilms International, 1979. Originally published by International Universities Press, 1946.

Pres, Terrence Des. *The Survivor: An Anatomy of Life in the Death Camps*. Oxford: Oxford University Press, 1976.

Prévost, Claude. "Entretien avec Charlotte Delbo." In *La Déportation dans la littérature et l'art: La Nouvelle Critique* 167 (Juin 1965): 41–44.

Raphael, Melissa: *Judaism and the Visual: A Post-Holocaust Theology of Jewish Art*. London/New York: Continuum International Publishing Group, 2009.

Ramadanovic, Petar. *Forgetting Futures On Memory, Trauma, and Identity*. Lanhan, MD: Lexington Books, 2001.

Rapaport, Herman. *Is There Truth in Art?* Ithaca and London: Cornell University Press, 1997.

Richert, Gerhard, ed. *Language without Soil: Adorno and Late Philosophical Modernity*. New York: Fordham University Press, 2010.

Robbins, Jill. *Altered Reading: Levinas and Literature*. Chicago and London: University of Chicago Press, 1999.

———, ed. *Is It Righteous to Be? Interviews with Emmanuel Levinas*. Stanford: Stanford University Press, 2002.

———. "Visage, Figure: Reading Levinas's 'Totality and Infinity.'" *Yale French Studies* 79 (1991).

Rose, Gillian. *Mourning Becomes the Law: Philosophy and Representation*. Cambridge: Cambridge University Press, 1996.

Rosenberg, Alan, and Gerald E. Meyers, eds. *Echoes from the Holocaust: Philosophical Reflections on a Dark Time*. Philadelphia: Temple University Press, 1988.

Rosenfeld, Alvin H. *A Double Dying: Reflections on Holocaust Literature*. Bloomington: Indiana University Press, 1980.

Roskies, David G. and Naomi Diamant. *Holocaust Literature. A History and Guide*. Waltham, MA: Brandeis University Press, 2012.

Roth, Michal S. *Memory, Trauma, and History. Essays on Living with the Past*. New York: Columbia University Press, 2012.

Rothberg, Michael. *Traumatic Realism: The Demands of Holocaust Representation*. Minneapolis and London: University of Minnesota Press, 2000.

Santner, Eric. *Stranded Objects: Mourning, Memory, and Film in Postwar Germany*. Ithaca, NY: Cornell University Press, 1990.

———. *On the Psychotheology of Everyday Life: Reflections on Freud and Rosenzweig*. Chicago: The University of Chicago Pres, 1996.

Santner, L. Gilman and Jack Zipes, eds. *Jewish Writing and Thought in German Culture, 1096–1996*. New Haven and London: Yale University Press, 1997.

Sars, Paul. "Poetry after Auschwitz: Paul Celan's Aesthetics of Hermetism." In *Contemporary Portrayals of Auschwitz: Philosophical Challenges*. Edited by Alan Rosenberg, James R. Watson, and Detlef Linke. Amherst, New York: Humanity Books, 2000.

Scarry, Elaine. *The Body in Pain: The Making and Unmaking of the World*. New York: Oxford University Press, 1985.

Scholem, Gershom. *Kabbalah*. New York: Quadrangle/New York Times Book Co., 1974.

Schumacher, Claude. "Charlotte Delbo: Le théatre comme moyen de survie." In *Créer pour survivre*. Actes du colloque international de l'université de Reims. Paris: Fédération Nationale des Déportés, Internés, Résistants et Patriotes, 1995.

———, ed. *Staging the Holocaust: The Shoah in Drama and Performance*. Cambridge: Cambridge University Press, 1998.

Semprun, Jorge. *L'ecriture et la vie*. Paris: Gallimard, 1994.

Seng, Joachim. *Auf den Kreis-Wegen der Dichtung: Zyklische Komposition bei Paul Celan am Beispiel der Gedichtbände bis "Sprachgitter."* Heidelberg: Universitätsverlag C. Winter, 1998.

Shoham, Chaim and Bernd Witte, hrsg. *Datum und Zitat bei Paul Celan.* In Akten des Internationalen Paul-Celan Colloquiums Haifa 1986.Bd. 21, Jahrbuch für internationale Germanistik, Reihe A. Kongressberichte. Bern, Frankfurt, New York, Paris: Peter Lang, 1987.

Smock, Ann. "Disastrous Responsibility." *L'Esprit Créateur* 24, no. 3 (1984): 5–20.

Spargo, Clifton R. *Vigilant Memory: Emmanuel Levinas, the Holocaust, and the Unjust Death.* Baltimore: Johns Hopkins University, 2006.

———, and Robert M. Ehrenreich. eds. *After Representation? The Holocaust, Literature and Culture.* New Brunswick: Rutgers University Press, 2010.

Sparr, Thomas. *Celans Poetik des hermetischen Gedichts.* Heidelberg: Carl Winter, 1989.

Spitzer, Leo. *After Babel: Aspects of Language and Translation.* New York: Oxford University Press, 1975.

Stewart, Corbet. "Paul Celan's Mode of Silence: Some Observations on 'Sprachgitter.'" *Modern Language Review* 67 (1972): 127–42.

Stewart Veronica. "Reading Trauma: Charlotte Delbo and the Struggle of Representation." In *Between the Psyche and the Polis: Refiguring History in Literature and Theory.* Edited by Michael Rossington and Anne Whitehead. Aldershot, UK: Ashgate, 2000.

Szondi, Peter. *Celan-Studien.* Frankfurt: Suhrkamp Verlag, 1972.

Thatcher, Nicole. *A Literary Analysis of Charlotte Delbo's Concentration Camp Re-Presentation.* Lewiston, NY: The Edwin Mellen Press, 1996.

Trezise, Thomas. "The Question of Community in Charlotte Delbo's Auschwitz and After." *MLN* 117 no.4 (2002): 858–66.

———. *Witnessing Witnessing: On the Reception of Holocaust Survivor Testimony.* New York: Fordham University Press, 2013.

Van der Kolk, Bessel A. and Onno Van der Hart. "The Intrusive Past: The Flexibility of Memory and the Engraving of Trauma." In *Trauma: Explorations in Memory.* Edited by Cathy Caruth. Baltimore and London: Johns Hopkins University Press, 1995.

Vansant, Jacqueline. *Reclaiming Heimat: Trauma and Mourning in Memoirs by Jewish Austrian Reémigrés.* Detroit: Wayne State University Press, 2001.

Virgil. *Aeneid.* Edited by Frederick M. Keener. Translated by John Dryden. London: Penguin Books, 1997.

Voswinckel, Klaus. *Paul Celan: Verweigerte Poetisierung der Welt. Versuch einer "Deutung."* Heidelberg: Lothar Stiehm Verlag, 1974.

Wernik Fridman, Lea. "Expression and Voice: Charlotte Delbo's 'None of Us Shall Return.'" In *Words and Witness: Narrative and Aesthetic Strategies in the Representation of the Holocaust.* New York: State University Press, 2000.

White, Hayden. *Tropics of Discourse: Essays in Cultural Criticism.* Baltimore and London: Johns Hopkins University Press, 1978.

Wieviorka, Annette. *Déportation et genocide: Entre la mémoire et l'oubli.* Paris: Plon, 1992.

———. *The Era of the Witness.* Ithaca: Cornell University Press, 2006.

Wills, David. *Prosthesis.* Meridian. Crossing Aesthetics. Edited by Werner Hamacher and David E. Wellbery. Stanford: Stanford University Press, 1995.

Wyschogrod, Edith. "Concentration Camps and the End of the Life-World." *Echoes from the Holocaust: Philosophical Reflections on a Dark Time.* Edited by Alan Rosenberg and Gerald E. Meyers. Philadelphia: Temple University Press, 1988.

Yildiz, Yasemin. *Beyond the Mother Tongue.* New York: Fordham University Press, 2012.

Young, James E. *Writing and Rewriting the Holocaust: Narrative and the Consequences of Interpretation.* Bloomington: Indiana University Press, 1988.

———. *The Texture of Memory: Holocaust Memorials and Meaning.* New Haven: Yale University Press, 1993.

———, ed. *The Art of Memory: Holocaust Memorials in History.* New York: Prestel, 1994.

————. *At Memory's Edge: After-Images of the Holocaust in Contemporary Art and Architecture.* New Haven and London: Yale University Press, 2000.

Ziarek, Krzystztof. *Inflected Language: Towards a Hermeneutics of Nearness: Heidegger, Levinas, Stevens, Celan.* SUNY Series in Continental Philosophy. Edited by Dennis J. Schmidt. Albany: State University of New York Press, 1994.

# Index

Abel, xxiv, 3–4, 24
Adorno, Theodor, 17n2, 43
Aladar, Elfer, 72
"Alice's Leg," xxvi, 51; call to participate, 65; effect on other female prisoners, 58, 59; grasping at meaning, 65; gypsy woman, 61; leg disappears, 60; life and death, 56, 59; present and past, 57; questions that arise, 56; reappearance of leg, 53–54; writing of, 62–65. *See also* Delbo, Charlotte
Alter, Robert, 4
annihilation, xiv, 30
Auschwitz-Birkenau, 49, 69, 70, 73, 76

Baer, Ulrich, 36, 43
Ball, Karyn, 32
Baumel, Judith Tydor, 70
Benjamin, Walter, xvi
Benveniste, Emile, 7
Bergen, Doris L., 71
Berger, John, 73
Blanchot, Maurice, 43
Braidotti, Rosi, 25
Bremen literature prize, 26–27
Buber, Martin, 7
Büchner, Georg, 35

Cain, xxiv, 4
Caruth, Cathy, xiv, xxii; memory, 52; trauma, 54, 55, 59
Celan, Paul, xiii, xxiii, xxv; biography, 23, 44n3; Bremen literature prize, 26; conflict with and attachment to the German language, 24–30, 32; as German poet, 22, 25; idea of time, 37; importance of mother tongue, 24, 31; as a Jew, 31, 40; mother as a theme, 31–32; ownership of language, 29, 30; poetry in light of Holocaust, 43. *See also* German language
Charcot, Jean-Martin, 52
Cixous, Hélène, 64
Clementi, Federica, 64, 71

dehumanization, xxi, 6, 70, 74–75, 79
Delbo, Charlotte, xiii, xxiii, xxvi; "Alice's Leg," 51, 53, 56–62; biography, 49; collective memory, 54; landscape of death, 57; memory theories, 51, 52; writing style, 52. *See also* "Alice's Leg"
Derrida, Jacques, xvi, xvii, xx, 28, 61
Des Pres, Terrence, xiii
Deutsch, Helene, 64
Diamant, Naomi, xiv
Dudach, Georges, 49

Eaglestone, Robert, xviii
ethical choices, 80–81
Eve, xxiv, 2–3, 6, 9; as mother of Cain and Abel, 7, 12, 14; legacy, 13–14; suffering and obligation, 13; telling her story, 7. *See also* mothers/motherhood
Ezrahi, Sidra Dekoven, xv, xxiv, 4

Felstiner, John, xiv, 2, 25
Fortunoff Video Archive for Holocaust Testimony, 3
French language, 28, 42, 60
Fynsk, Christopher, 30

gender, xiii, xx, xxiii, xxvi, 13; assaults on female body, 74–75, 80; difference of female and male experiences, 69, 71, 78; and fascism, 75–76; ideas of manliness, 75–76;

nakedness and nudity, 72–73;
    structure of, xix, xxvi. *See also*
    mothers/motherhood
German language, xxv, 2, 27;
    complicity of, 27, 37; cultural
    traditions, 29, 40, 47n71; language
    and meaning, 36; language of
    oppression v. language of
    expression, 24, 25, 26, 30, 34;
    violence to, 29. *See also* Celan, Paul;
    language
Ginsburg, Yitzchack, 14, 19n34
Glowacka, Dorota, xviii, 6, 80
Goertz, Karein, 51
Goldenberg, Myra, xxiv, 64, 71, 77
Greenspan, Henry, xxii
Grese, Irma, xv, 78
gypsy woman, 61. *See also* "Alice's
    Leg"

Hamacher, Werner, 41, 43
Hartman, Geoffrey, 43
Hedgepeth, Sonja Maria, 71
Herder, Johann Gottfried, 24
Hirsch, Marianne, 24, 64, 71
Holocaust Studies, xxii, xxiv
Horowitz, Sara, xxiii, xxiv, 69, 78
Humboldt, Wilhelm von, 24
Hutton, Christopher, 27
"Ideal Aryan," 75, 76

Irigaray, Luce, 64
"I/you," 3, 19n24, 32, 39, 45n40; and
    narrative positive, 7; transit witness,
    8

Janet, Pierre, 52
Jewish teaching and identity, 14, 16
Johnson, Barbara, xx, 7, 24, 32
Joris, Pierre, 26
Jouvet, Louis, 49

Kacandes, Irene, 7
Kafka, Franz, 24
Kapezius, Dr., 77
Kaplan, Ann, xxii
Kaplan, Brett Ashley, xviii, 50
Kaplan, Marion, 71
Katz, Claire, xix

Klein, Fritz, 71, 73
Konz, Claudia, 71
Kremer, S. Lillian, 71
Kristeva, Julia, 25, 64

Lacan, Jacques, 34
LaCapra, Dominick, 8
Lacoue-Labarthe, Philipp, 27
Langbein, Herman, xxii
Langer, Lawrence, 50
language, xiv, xxii, 28; Celan's poetry,
    43; crisis within, 59; importance of,
    xxv; pertaining to "Alice's Leg," 59,
    63; poetry as link between language
    and memory, 31, 35–36; power of, 5;
    theory of, 29. *See also* French
    Language; German language
Laska, Vera, 71
Laub, Dori, xxi
Lengyel, Miklós, 72
Lengyel, Olga, xiii, xiv, xxiii, xxvi, 69;
    biography, 70, 72; fate of sons, 72–73
Levinas, Emmanuel, xviii–xxii, 73, 80
Levine, Michael G., 3
Lower, Wendy, 71
Lyotard, Jean François, xvi, xx, 43

memory, xiv, xvii, xx, xxii, 50, 61;
    "Alice's Leg," 61; blurring of, 69;
    Cain and Abel story, 4; Celan and
    language, 33; collective, 54; Eve and
    narrative, 7, 12; inability to
    comprehend, 55, 56, 68n47; Pagis
    and, 12; role of poetry, 34, 39;
    studies on, 52. *See also* testimony;
    trauma
Mengele, Josef, xv, xxvi, 71, 77, 78,
    79–80
Meyers, Carol, 9
Milton, Sybil, 74
Mosse, George, 75–76
mothers/motherhood, xviii, xix,
    xxviiin23; as affirmation of life, xx,
    12, 17, 43; assault upon, 15–16;
    creating a home, 11, 13, 14; images
    of, xx; in landscape of death, 38;
    mother and child, 3, 34, 68n57, 78; as
    nourishment, 64; pregnant, xiv,
    xxvi, 69, 76–77, 79–80; source of

Jewishness, 10–11; in "Sprich auch Du," 32; victims of Nazi annihilation, 10; as witness, 4, 24. *See also* Eve

mother tongue, xx, xxv, 24; importance of, 23–24, 32, 40

Ofer, Dalia, 71
Oliver, Kelly, 33
"Other," the, xvii, xix, 8, 16, 28; appeal impossible, xxi; and child, 34; Eve's story, 8–9; and home, 14; link to the feminine, 64; obligations to, 16; self's responsibility for, xxi, 12, 13

Pajević, Marco, 35
Pagis, Dan, xiii, xxiii, xxiv, 1; use of allegory, 12; biography, 2; displacement, 4; Eve, Abel, and Cain, 4; and poetry, 1, 4; themes in work, 4, 6, 12; use of biblical characters, 4, 12. *See also* "Written in Pencil in a Sealed Railway-Car"
"patriarchal" hierarchy, xx
Patterson, David, 10–15
Perl, Gisella, xiii, xxiii, xxvi, 69; biography, 76–78
Pickford, Henry, xviii
Plank, Karl A., 5
prosthesis, 62

Ravensbrück, 49, 51
reading, xiv. *See also* writing
Ringelheim, Joan, 71
Ritter, Carol, 71
Roskies, David G., xiv
Roth, John, 71
Roth, Michael, xxiii, 50
Rothberg, Michael, xviii, 50; traumatic realism, 50–51
Rubin, Agi, xxii

Safdie, Moshe, 18n20

Saidel, Rochelle G., 71
Schleiermacher, Friedrich, 24
Shapiro, Amy, xxiv, 64, 71, 73
Sokoloff, Naomi, 4
Spargo, R. Clifton, 12–14
Steiner, George, 43
Stewart, Victoria, 53
Suleiman, Susan Rubin, 64
survival, xiii, xix, 38, 44; as affirmation of life, xvi, xxii; and "Other," xix; and poetic voice, 33–34
"Sprich auch Du," xxv, 31–32, 34

testimony, xiv, xvii, 36, 41, 62, 63, 69; figurative, 63–64; poetry and, 3, 33, 43; shifting perspectives, xxiv; survival, xxiv
Tobias, Rochelle, 37
trauma, 53, 58, 59, 68n62; of "Alice's Leg," 63; intersection of testimony and language, xxi; and language, 66n13, 67n38; repetition of, 58; traumatic realism, 50
"Ulysses Gramophone," xxii

Voswinckel, Klaus, 31

Wannsee Conference, 1
Weitzman, Leonore J., 71
Wieviorka, Annette, xiv
Wills, David, 62
writing, xiii, xvi, xviii, 8; as act of survival, xvii, xviii, xxii–xxiii, 57; effect on readers, xv; gender differences, xix, xx; and memory, 39; and mother tongue, 24; narrative and poetry, 17n2, 40
"Written in Pencil in the Sealed Railway-Car," xiv, xxiv; analysis, 1, 2–4; Eve's voice, 2; as testimony, 5

Yildiz, Yasemin, 24–25, 43

# About the Author

**Petra M. Schweitzer** received her PhD in Comparative Literature from Emory University. She is currently teaching at Shenandoah University in Winchester, Virginia. Her scholarly work and teaching include Comparative Literature, French, and German, with a specialization in Holocaust studies, memory, testimony, and trauma studies. Additionally, she teaches First Year Seminar courses with a concentration on Global Genocide studies.

Lightning Source UK Ltd.
Milton Keynes UK
UKHW010342050719
345200UK00024BA/485/P